THE RIPPLES

WHAT LIES BEYOND

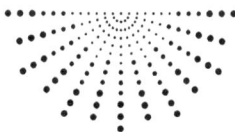

DANIELLE AITKEN

PHP

Please note: This is a work of fiction. Characters, places and incidents are fictitious. Any resemblance to people, places or real situations are purely coincidental.

www.danielleaitkenauthor.com.au

NATIONAL LIBRARY OF AUSTRALIA

A catalogue record of this book is available from: www.trove.nla.gov.au

ISBN (print): 978-0-6488078-0-3

ISBN (eBook) : 978-0-6488078-1-0

Editor: Susan Wakefield

Proofreader: Helen Batziris

Cover Design: Project Heart Publishing

Cover Photograph: Shutterstock Images

Interior design: Project Heart Publishing

Print typesetting and eBook productions: Vellum

ACKNOWLEDGMENTS

This book is dedicated to my beautiful family, many of whom have been directly touched by the ongoing and ever-present effects of suicide in many ways.

Special Acknowledgements to:

Brandon Bartolomei
Morgan McNabb
Nicole McAtear
Lachlan McNabb
Georgina Park
Rachel Aitken

Also to Phillip Aitken who continues to support me in all of my endeavours.

I am forever grateful.

* * *

I also acknowledge

Any of you reading this book who have been affected by the relentless damaging impacts of a calamitous event.

You know who you are.

DEDICATION

To All Those Lost
&
To All Those Saved

WHAT PEOPLE ARE SAYING

THE RIPPLES

This is the gripping account of one family's experience of suicide, and the ripple effects that radiate out of this most desperate of all human tragedies. Aitken bravely delves into the world of suicide to explore its social, emotional, familial, moral, political and institutional origins and ramifications, and tightly weaves the impacts of suicide (and its after-effects) upon not only a family in crisis but an entire community and beyond. With careful sensitivity, she unpacks both the nature of suicide and its causes, in an effort to shine a light on this increasingly prevalent modern epidemic. With deft compassion and resolve, Aitken tackles the troubling aspects of the human condition linked to the hard issues surrounding suicide, and shows us how to make sense of the unthinkable through the powerful, redemptive forces of love, offering ways as to how we can actively become part of the solution.

Susan Wakefield

Freelance Writer, Novelist and published Poet, who has worked as an editor and proofreader for various publications including 'The Boston Globe' and 'The New York Times".

***

Danielle Aitken has written a masterpiece here, with the utmost respect to one of life's most tragic acts.

The Ripples is a stunning piece of writing revealing the painful ripples, floating over not only the entire family tortured in their grief for a lost child, but an entire community and beyond.

Aitken has weaved a powerful story of love, loss and a journey that makes each and everyone of us question and ask, why? If only, and what if?

Aitken has touched on thought provoking topics throughout the book, that will certainly be both enlightening and a warm hug to many individuals; and certainly those that have been touched by the heartbreak of suicide.

Although I cried my way through most of this book, it was with absolute wonder and respect to the human heart and soul, to how much one can continue to bear after being impacted with such loss, and still survive in a world without a loved one.

I was in absolute awe with the sensitivity and beauty that Aitken has written about Mark Frederick and his thought process, and his journey looking on after his decision was made and carried out.

Move over Jodi Picoult, Danielle Aitken is on the rise.

Michelle Weitering

Author of Thirteen and Underwater.

***

"Suicide is so often a taboo topic, yet Danielle Aitken fearlessly takes on the challenge of writing about the ripple effects of a life lost too soon. This modern-day story explores the darkest corners of a family struggling with grief and their inability to prevent slipping into a dysfunctional abyss after tragedy rips through their home. Tackling marriage separation, teenage drugs, and the dependency so many youths have on social media to provide the 'feel good' factor, the author deals with the unraveling of a community when death takes one of their own. An important book to open up more dialogue in society around mental health awareness, suicide prevention, and the importance of reaching out for support when life's complications become overwhelming."

Kelly Van Nelson

Poet and Amazon bestselling Author of Graffiti Lane, and Punch & Judy

I WONDER WHAT WE WOULD CHOOSE

***

If we could see the impact of our actions before we took them,

I wonder what we would choose.

If, for a split second, we had the precious gift of wisdom in
that moment before we acted,

I wonder what we would choose.

If that split second in time spoke to us of how important,
needed and truly loved we really were,

I wonder what we would choose.

If that single pivotal moment of clarity was ours to observe,

I wonder what we would choose.

If we truly knew just how far the ripples of our actions would
reach, and how they would continue to erode away at all of
those we leave behind, just like the relentless erosion of waves
crashing onto a sandy shore long after the storm has passed,

I wonder what we would choose.

***

Danielle Aitken

TABLE OF CONTENTS

1. The End

2. What Went Wrong?

3. Calamity

4. Mark

5. The Morning After the Day Before

6. The Ripple Becomes A Tsunami

7. The Unseen Casualties

8. Mr. Gregory Preston

9. The Students Unite

10. Christine: The Decline

11. Alex: Life Goes On

12. The Promotion

13. The Psychological Toll Continues

14. Take My Hand

15. Drowning Not Waving

16. And So It Goes

17. The Beginning

THE END

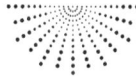

7:05am Monday the 18th March.

It was the beginning of another excruciatingly intolerable week, but this week would be different.

Today the weight of those excruciating feelings and those intolerable thoughts had finally become too much to bear. The pressures he had been enduring, unobserved by those closest to him, could no longer be carried by this 18-year-old boy—*or was he now a young man?* He wasn't sure. This thought had perplexed him, sometimes a boy, sometimes a man, depending on the observer and their agendas. How was he supposed to know which role to assume as he navigated the territory of being an adolescent?

To all those looking on, he appeared to be very successful; a school captain, a talented football player, a state champion runner, a straight 'A' student. Yet, these and many other things had contributed to the insurmountable emotional burden that was now overwhelming.

He was resolved on his next course of action.

The days where his mind had been screaming for relief had now passed.

He was finally peacefully numb...it was precious relief at last.

He had been a body just going through the perfunctory actions of existence, but, mercifully he now knew, it was not for much longer. The peace he had yearned for was now mere moments away.

Life had become so difficult for him; and now, at this pivotal moment of surrender he truly believed that his family and friends would be better off without the heavy burden of the person he had become; he was nothing more than a troubled, tormented, emotional mess. They would be shocked initially, he reasoned, but they would move on.

He had thought long and hard about this moment. He had wondered if any of them would later consider the impact of their harsh words, or the effect of the anonymous messages from faceless strangers that flashed on his screens at all hours of the day and night. Most of these pernicious attacks were punishment for the blameless sins of his fortunate genetics; he was talented, good at so many things. He was a tall poppy, and this was not allowed. You were permitted to struggle. That was okay. You were allowed to be '*not too bad,*' but if you excelled at any one thing you drew attention to yourself; and this was seen to be showing off. Mark Fredrick was certainly not a show off, far from it in fact. However, he was not just excelling at one thing; he excelled at most things.

He had wondered if they would understand the pressure he had carried. The pressure from some, to not be *too* good at any given thing, which conflicted with the constant pressure from others to succeed in *all* things. Both expectations had been a heavy load for him to carry.

He had wondered if they would understand that those who said they were his friends, were the very same ones who had deserted him or criticised him in the moments he needed them most. He wondered if they had any awareness that they had hurt him more than they could ever know.

He had wondered if they would understand that he too, was just trying to survive, all the while feeling as though he was drowning; slowly being dragged under by the heavy weight of life's invisible burdens.

He had wondered if they could understand the deep despair he felt and the total loss of hope, that greeted him at the beginning of each day, and met with him every night in the darkness of his room.

He had wondered if they would even care, or would they be so caught up in their own lives that they would hardly notice his absence?

Now, however, all such thoughts had left him.

At this crucial and defining moment he was at last, peacefully numb.

Mark Fredrick stood emotionless in his room at that critical moment, on that pivotal day, that would for ever-after define him. He was aware that his mother was downstairs. She would be checking her emails while getting his younger siblings, Jessica and Hannah, ready for school. He had fifteen minutes before anyone would be looking for him. Fifteen minutes was enough time, he thought.

He stood motionless, unable to think, unable to feel. He was weighed down by an unprecedented despair, and this heaviness was now finally overwhelming him. His ongoing attempts to deal with all of this on his own were now totally exhausted and seemed futile. It was a relief to know he no longer needed to try.

But Mark had no way of knowing that his next action would create a trail of destruction that would be so far reaching that it would go on, and on, and on; just like ripples created in the absolute stillness of a mirror-perfect body of water, after an unprecedented impact disturbs the calm forever.

He had no idea just how far reaching the ripples he was about to set in motion would flow, and for how long. Nor was he in any emotional state to care. Logic had long since left him. He was now somehow just going through the motions of an existence that no longer seemed to be his own.

Relief was beckoning to him and was now so vivid a prospect that he had lost his capacity to reason.

He looked at the noose fastened to the overhead beam, which he would soon hold in his clammy hands for the last time.

The sound of his own heartbeat threatened to deafen him.

Boom Boom

Boom Boom

Boom Boom

No thoughts.

Peace at last.

Seconds felt like hours.

Boom Boom

Boom Boom

Boom Boom

His mind was mercifully numb.

In a trance, he stepped up onto the stool and for the last time, stared at the noose in his hand as he secured it around his own neck without feeling.

He took one emotionless step forward and everything familiar to him vanished from view.

He was aware of the ticking of the clock on the wall reminding him of the precious seconds that were passing by, moment to moment.

There was a fleeting instant, a mere flicker in time, almost as soon as his feet left the stool, when the terrible thought crossed his mind: "*Oh God what have I done?*"

Suddenly, silence.

The clock and his deafening heart beat stopped and time stood still.

* * *

Mark stood by the door of his bedroom. He felt lighter than he had felt in years. The heavy emotions that had weighed him down had vanished as if by magic, and had been replaced with an over-whelming feeling that he had previously never experienced.

The clock on the wall was declaring it was 7.08 am and all was silent and still.

In front of him he could see his lifeless body, almost as though frozen in time, hanging from the noose that, not minutes before, he had placed around his own neck just seconds before he stepped off the upturned stool that was now lying on the floor beneath his dangling feet. Surprisingly, this vision did not frighten or disturb him in any way. There was a surreal stillness around him. He seemed to be having an out of body experience and all he could feel in this extraordinary moment was complete and utter peace.

The total disconnection from his body and his old life was bemusing but not at all concerning. He was aware that he *should* feel something about the fact that his body was hanging there in front of him, but he didn't. He just felt...*Love. Was it love? Yes, definitely Love.*

He had read about such things in his psychology readings, but he never really believed they were possible. He had thought such accounts were nothing more than the ramblings of crazy people, or the neurological delusions of an oxygen deprived brain, struggling to hold on to reality. That must be what this was. The delusions of *his* oxygen deprived brain. He thought that realisation should actually

5

disturb him, but the truth was that it did not. He was now nothing more than an observer filled with euphoria. He pondered that for a moment. *Was this euphoria? he mused, or was it the purest feeling of love? or were they one and the same?* He was unsure, but he pondered the similarities between these emotions until his musings were interrupted by a growing awareness of another unearthly presence in the room.

As Mark became more aware of this celestial presence, the likes of which he had never seen or even imagined, he remained extraordinarily calm. Nothing could upset him right now.

He was in a state of pure acceptance.

The presence seemed to be an embodiment of pure love that radiated out from the very core of its form in every direction, creating a warmth and serenity in the previously overwhelming atmosphere of his bedroom. Its form seemed to be changing with his growing awareness of its presence. He again noticed with surprise that he was in no way disturbed by this evolving apparition, which he believed must be an angel of sorts. He felt only deep comfort and love, and an all-encompassing warmth, which radiated through his entire essence.

To be truthful, Mark knew very little about angels, or even God—and right about now, the alive Mark that he had been not five minutes ago would probably have been berating himself for not paying more attention in religious education classes. To be fair, he could never have imagined that he would ever be faced with a situation like this one, but nonetheless, here he was, or was not; he really wasn't sure. He was yet to make sense of exactly what or where this was, and interestingly, once again, it did not concern him at all.

His family were not especially religious; in fact, he really wasn't sure of what he actually believed in, but apparently this was a moot point as the evolving presence began to take on the more familiar form of a young woman who was radiating a heavenly, welcoming, somewhat warming light energy, the likes of which his earthly vocabulary could not adequately describe.

He thought without concern that this beautiful ethereal presence must surely be here to guide him to heaven. He hoped he would be going to heaven. Why else would she be here? Surely if he were to be going somewhere else, somewhere, shall we say 'less pleasant,' he would not be feeling like this—or would he?

His thoughts were interrupted.

'We are not going to Heaven,' she communicated to him without speaking a word; in fact, he had not spoken either. She must be reading his mind, he again thought without concern, as he immediately became aware that he had just read hers too. Confused now, he wondered how this could be.

She smiled at him, a heavenly smile that expressed to him that he would soon understand.

"I am Grace. You are safe. I am here. I have always been here."

This time she actually spoke to him as her form continued to become more earthly in appearance and less transparent. His form was also still somehow his own, despite the fact he could clearly see his body hanging directly in front of him.

He looked at her and immediately felt her loving warmth. He instinctively knew, she was here for him. In that moment it became clear to him. In an instant, he knew what he had always yearned to know. He was loved, *truly, truly loved*. This love did not come from his friends or family; this love was untarnished and was the purest of pure love; an unconditional love that he now recognised was eternal. He also instinctively began to understand something else in that moment; he was not alone. In fact, Mark was now beginning to comprehend that he had *never* been alone. Even in his darkest moments of despair, he now understood that this exceptional being of pure love and pure light had been beside him always. What a difference it would have made to have known and understood this, he thought.

He pondered those eight little words which he now recognised carried the most enormous potential to save so many lives: *You are loved. You are never ever alone.*

A pang of sudden remorse and regret flooded through him as the implications of his musings became apparent.

Oh my God, what have I done?

2

WHAT WENT WRONG

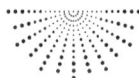

M ark was a champion athlete, it had always been that way, as long as he could remember. His high level of performance and proficiency in any given sport he turned his hand to often allowed him to run faster, jump higher or kick farther than the best athletes in the state.

His football ability ensured he was a most sought-after player whose mere presence on the team generally guaranteed a win. To onlookers, Mark appeared to take this all in his stride, but there was another side to Mark, a side that for the most part was hidden from view. A part that carried the expectation of family, friends, school companions and even local community members. Yes, success came easily for him in one regard, but in another way it was incredibly difficult. It was expected by most that he *would* win, after all, he was Mark Fredrick, of course he would win; he always won. It was inevitable, but this success came with a heavy price tag. There were those who would have preferred to see Mark fail. Those people who in some way felt threatened by all of his success. Some were fellow athletes from his own athletic squad or football team, or worse, some were athletes' family members, who actually wanted to see him fail.

Although Mark tried to ignore this undercurrent of added pressure, it had started to take its toll.

He was seldom beaten, that is true, but he never assumed success, and he never took his elite athleticism for granted. He felt the burden of expectation riding heavily on his shoulders, and as such, he often went into a race with multiple fears: *What if he did get beaten? What if this time he lost? Who would he be letting down and what would they think?* They were all relying on him; no—losing was not an option for Mark Fredrick...*but what if he did*?

He trained hard, almost as though his very life depended on it, and, for him, perhaps it did. Training was his safety net, a necessary obsession required to take him all the way to the highest level of athletic success. He had always qualified for the Australian Athletic National Championships, ever since he was 13 years of age. He truly was a 'natural' and he had a passion for sport of all kinds. He was captain of the regional football team for his age group and he often played up one or even two age groups. This past season he captained the U18 team to the grand final and played several games with the seniors. However, the football season was now long behind him, and he was heavily involved in Athletics Victoria's most serious and competitive end of the season.

Mark had already qualified for Nationals by medalling in the State Championships. There was not a year that had gone by that he had *not* medalled. His natural ability had always served him well, but Mark never assumed anything. His coach trained him hard.

"You can't be complacent, Mark, there will always be someone nipping at your heels; Jimmy Sutherland is just a tenth of a second behind you," he would often say as he sent Mark on another round of interval training or back into the gym. Mark did not even know who Jimmy Sutherland was, but he suspected he may have been the boy who came out of nowhere to steal the gold away from Coach Oaks back in 1989.

Mark had already achieved the qualifying standards for the upcoming national competition. All he had to do was show up to the Victorian championships, and his place at the Australian National Track and Field Championships was assured, but Mark was never one to just get by. He always did his best. He never took it for granted that he would win, even though he usually did. His team mates were very supportive and cheered him on to all of his successes, but for Mark there was another story playing in his mind, just beneath the surface. He had been feeling an increasing amount of pressure to achieve. His loving parents and grandparents would make little comments that were meant to support and rally him on, like *"PB today Mark?" "Run fast Mark," "Just do your best."* Even comments like *"do your best"* came with an unintended but much weightier meaning when you were national champion. It all really meant the same thing; *win Mark.*

You are the best...

Your PB is the record...

Do better than the record...

Break the record...

Do better...

Go faster...

Win...

He knew they didn't mean it that way, but what if he couldn't do his best every time, what if he couldn't reach his Personal Best? He knew it wasn't even possible to PB in every event, but nonetheless here he was, expected to always 'do his best.' At some point you must reach the point of *'as good as it gets'* and what then? What if he never PB'ed again?

His coach and some of the other members of the squad all offered their support in various ways that were never meant to add to this young man's burdens, but the unintended consequences of this praise on a boy who was the highest of achievers was felt all the same.

Mark never acknowledged the degree of pressure weighing on him in this area of his life because most of it actually came from Mark himself.

He wanted his family to be proud, he wanted to win for his school, for his community, for his state—and eventually for his country. He wanted to be school captain and to lead his football team to victory, but at some point the scales of balance began to tip.

Year Twelve, although only just beginning, had its own requirements, as again Mark felt he needed to succeed at the highest of levels to gain the ATAR score that would allow him to follow his dreams.

Strangers would often stop him in the street to congratulate him or wish him well. Unbeknownst to them, this added another layer to the burden of being Mark Fredrick. He often appeared in the local paper, with headings such as "Local Hero Brings Home the Gold" or "Young Athlete Headed for Tokyo." The community banded together and held fundraisers for him to help finance his travel as he held the hopes and dreams of so many.

For most, Mark was the popular 'feel good' news story in an ocean of bad news which people were looking for. There were also the others, who were not so generous with their words or support. The insensitive comments by faceless strangers, who felt the need to comment on Mark personally, often extreme to the point of being malicious. These comments seemed to coincide with the media exposure he was getting. It seemed the more success he achieved, the more he was singled out and the greater the backlash.

He was also targeted by those who thought the community should not be funding a boy to go to another country for sport while the farmers were struggling through terrible drought, or the country was recovering from the worst bushfires in history, or greenhouse gas emissions were contributing to global warming. Mark's potential pending trip, which at this point had not even been confirmed by the selection committee, was apparently affecting all these global issues.

In an attempt to escape the cumulative strains being exerted on him, Mark found increasing solace in his ability to lose himself, and the world at large, by disappearing into the cyber-world of social media. Here he could be Mark, just Mark, for a while at least. However, it didn't take long for the internet trolls to find him and stalk him there. The 'bullying' that ensued came at Mark in many ways, not least of which was through social media platforms and chat rooms. He was singled out, constantly taunted or mocked for being too confident, by those who thought they had the right to say hurtful things to a young man they did not even know. Some would criticise him for being too good while others would launch the most vicious attacks accusing him of being useless or not good enough. Some would tell him to give it up and let someone else with more talent have a go. The attacks were relentless. Most often Mark tried to ignore them, but the fact was each one of these taunts was having a cumulative effect on Mark, consistently whittling away at his self-esteem and self-confidence, and eventually beating him down until he arrived at a place of self-loathing from which he could see no escape.

For Mark, social media quickly turned from a welcome escape from the real world to something he could no longer escape, as the relent-lessness of it followed him day and night. Nowhere was he immune to the insidiousness of its reach. It plagued him even in the middle of the night, in the sanctity of his own bedroom. The hateful posts were something to behold.

For some, Mark was becoming something akin to a villain, though guilty of nothing more than the sins of his success. He was too good at too much; he was *too* successful. He was even *too* good looking. Guilty of the sins of his genetics, he became a slave to the chat rooms and the social media channels that commented on sport and all things Mark Fredrick. He didn't even know when this began, but there was a definite ground swell of Mark Fredrick haters that had seemed to materialise out of nowhere; everyone had something to say. His schooling, even his athletics, began to suffer as he spent more and more time in his room, sinking into the cyber cesspool of online negativity. A world in which he could never win.

The tide was definitely turning for Mark, as he hopelessly attempted to swim against it. Silently and unobserved, exhaustion and depression ensued, as he attempted in vain to maintain control in a world where control was an impossibility. The one thing that was becoming obvious was the worse he felt the more compelled he was to return to the cyber world of un-reality, in a sense to protect himself, because in this world there was no other sentinel. There were no parents, there was no coach, there was no principal, there was just him and a world of faceless strangers. Here he had to be his own keeper, he had to stand guard 24/7 —and it was an exhausting task. This was a world of bullies and tormentors. It was a world that most adults were completely unaware of, but this was the world Mark Fredrick found himself heavily impacted by, and in the worst possible ways.

Now the thing with young people is that they do not have the life skills to deal with the many negative, complex effects of social media. They can often find themselves being compared to the unrealistic expectations of the 'Social media world' demands that are completely unachievable. However, when you are so caught up in the cyber world that your connection with the real world becomes unclear—as it was for Mark Fredrick—it is easy to find yourself slipping into a hopelessly dark place.

Mark had always considered himself to be a smart young man, alert to the pitfalls of life, but in fact he, like many teenagers, was completely unaware of the warning signs. The more he entered the cyber world, the more he began to lose interest in schooling and sport, both unprecedented issues for Mark. The more he continued to disconnect from real life, the more isolated and irritable he became. He was even sometimes hostile towards those who did not understand what he was going through. Arguing for the first time ever with his best friend, Hamish McKinley, led Mark to break all ties with him when he really needed him the most.

Over the previous months Mark had become more and more emotional; tearful on many occasions as he read and reread the hate posts. *"You're a loser Fredrick,"* or *"Give it up and let someone with talent have a go."* The taunts went on and on, someone even once said, *"Fuck off and die Fredrick."* He felt it difficult to get any perspective about these issues. School was suffering, everything was suffering. He knew his mother had noticed, but he shrugged her off whenever she asked if he was ok. He *was* ok, he thought. He just no longer felt like eating with the family; in fact he really no longer felt like eating at all. Lack of sleep intensified everything and over time left him only semi-functioning in a foggy haze that further compounded his lack of ability to reason. Depression and low self-esteem ensued, but as with many teens, his ability to compensate, at least for a while, allowed his symptoms to remain hidden from view. After all, he was Mark Fredrick, the highest of achievers. If there were changes in his behaviour, most would just put it down to the adaptations required to navigate a very stressful year ahead. But what they did not know was to change the path of all of their lives forever.

If only Mark Fredrick had known before his death that social media is now being recognised throughout the world by many experts as the biggest contributing factor to adolescent depression.

If only he had known that, between 2009 and 2017, the rates of severe depression and suicide in the 14 to 17 year-old age group had spiralled out of control, increasing by up to 60% in some countries.

If only he had been aware of the interesting connection between the implementation and massive over usage of social media platforms by this age group, during the very same period of time, he *may* have been alerted to the signs.

If only he *had* been aware of the signs in the first place.

If only people had told him, educated him, warned him.

If only he had known that this was but a moment in time that he would get through, and life would eventually be okay again.

If only he had known, but he did not know.

How could he have known the path he was on, unseen by others, would be a catastrophic one for him and everyone who knew him?

How *could* he have known?

3

CALAMITY

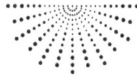

C hristine was downstairs dressed impeccably, ready for her day. Her hair was pulled back by a loose tortoise shell clip and perfectly positioned, which served to highlight her high cheek bones and her beautifully long neck.

Today, she wore a navy tight, figure-hugging skirt that complemented her shapely body, an embroidered white blouse which was perfectly pressed and expensive leather shoes. There was never to be any compromise when it came to shoes. According to Christine, the comfort of one's feet could make all the difference between a property being passed in, or sold at auction in a successful sale.

Others were often envious of her; even after four pregnancies Christine had managed to keep an exceptional figure; this however, was no accident. Christine worked hard to achieve success in all areas of her life. She *was* a high achiever and her rigorous exercise routine and healthy vegetarian diet were no exceptions.

She was an attractive woman, self-assured and composed. A woman who exuded an air of competence in all that she did. There was a certain irresistible charm about her that was undeniable, and Christine was not opposed to using this to her advantage when she was closing on a sale. She was always striving to get the best possible price for her vendors and she took this responsibility very seriously. Of course, the increased commission she personally received due to the inflated sale price was an added bonus that served to keep Christine hungry for the maximum price. She *was* competitive, there was no denying it.

She was the senior agent at McGregor's, the local and most successful real estate agency in the south eastern suburbs. McGregor's was situated conveniently just three minutes' drive from their very own well-appointed, centrally located double story five-bedroom home with in ground pool. It suited her growing family well and would be an easy home to sell, if she and Alexander ever chose to sell it, although right now she could never imagine doing such a thing. This was an amazing family home, perfect for her maturing family and met all their social needs.

Christine always encouraged the children to have their friends over. For her, it was far better to know where they were and whom they were with. She could never understand parents who allowed their children to wander the streets. This was definitely not her way at all as a parent. She enjoyed maintaining a degree of control over her children's activities and although she allowed them a certain amount of independence, it was always measured and well considered. She wasn't what you would call an overbearing mother; she was just a very busy woman and as competent at child rearing as she was at selling property—and a certain degree of control was the key to her success.

This had been Christine and Alex's family home now for nineteen years. They had moved in from their small one-bedroom studio apartment after discovering that Christine was pregnant with their first child, Mark. She and Alex were newly married, and having children had not exactly been on Christine's to-do list at the time. She had a career to establish first, but, as she rapidly became accustomed to the growing life within her, the thought of *not* having this baby never occurred to her.

Always adaptable, Christine set about planning for their rapidly changing future. She was a young estate agent back then, just starting out. How different life had been, so carefree. Of course, there was not so much of the confidence and certainly not so much of the competence that now imbued her every business interaction, but nonetheless, these years were akin to her 'university of life.' She always looked back on these times fondly, and she was very aware that she would not be where she was today without these life lessons.

Alex and Christine had met at a party many years ago, when Christine was only twenty. Alex was twenty-five and had just arrived back from six months in the United States. Their chance meeting may very well never have happened if not for Alex's older brother Stephen, dragging his jet-lagged brother Alex out that night. "Can't hibernate forever," Stephen had said as he enthusiastically guided his very tired brother towards the waiting car.

Christine also could have quite easily missed out on attending the party that evening if not for the insistence of *her* best friend, Cathy.

The two seemed destined to be together, and, almost from the moment they first met their future together seemed fated. It had been a whirlwind romance after that initial chance meeting, that they now both knew may just as easily never have happened.

Alexander was comfortably confident within himself. The presence of a strong woman was something that excited him. He loved to watch Christine shine in her own spectacular way in business and at home. Five years older than Christine, he had already completed a law degree when he decided to travel to Europe and the United States for six months. He was coming back to a job with a law firm as a junior employee, when he and Christine chanced to meet at that party; twenty-three years later, here they were. How long ago that all seemed now.

They had been so well suited and life had been easy for them. Now both parents expertly managed busy work schedules whilst maintaining a happy family-life balance. There was a love and a bond between them that to the outside world seemed indestructible; the perfect couple, the perfect marriage.

The trials and tribulations of family life were sensitively navigated together. United in their cause, their joint parenting style supported independence while encouraging their children to participate in a wide variety of activities.

That fated morning, as she stood at her ergonomic desk, which was perfectly positioned to observe the morning movements of the family, she continued to check and respond to the Monday morning emails. She was aware that Mark had five more minutes to make an appearance before she would take the now quite familiar journey up the stairs herself to get him moving. This, she had noticed, was becoming more and more necessary over the past few weeks.

Mark usually needed no encouragement in the mornings to get up and be ready for school; in fact he was often up first to go for a run, or to do some last minute study for the day's exam. He was generally well prepared for all of his examinations, but he still took the extra time to review. His marks in his schoolwork had always reflected his diligence.

Christine had spoken to him about the recent changes in his behaviour that were becoming concerning to her, as she tried to rekindle his motivation.

"You're in your final year at school, Mark. The study is not going to happen on its own," she would say, but lately it seemed to be falling on deaf ears. She was aware that his assessment scores had begun to slip over the last month. He seemed to be unconcerned about this whenever she broached the subject with him. He had always been a straight 'A' student, he had always cared about his scores, but something had changed, and it was out of character for him. Part of her hoped it was just a time of adjustment. He had taken on more responsibilities at the school, but she had begun to feel uneasy about it. She had asked him on more than one occasion if everything was all right. He had assured her that he was fine, but there *was* something different. She couldn't quite put her finger on what, but she had definitely noticed it. She was a great believer in maternal instinct and generally didn't ignore it. She had meant to speak to Alex about it over the weekend but Hannah had been unwell, and Jessica had boy issues, so the opportunity never arose. She would just have to speak to him tonight, she thought.

Hannah was the youngest of the siblings. She had been watching morning TV as she ate her breakfast at the breakfast bar, always under Christine's watchful eye. The morning routine was scheduled so that everything was done in a timely fashion, and today was no exception. Hannah was now eight years old and in grade three at school. She had a special kind of love for animals of every kind. She loved to take photos of them, read about them, and watch anything she could on TV about them. Most of all she just wanted to be around them whenever she could. Even at her tender young age, Hannah was sure about her future. To nobody's surprise she had already decided that she wanted a life surrounded by animals; she wanted to be a vet. She thought this would be a wonderful job, but, for Hannah, it really felt more like a calling. Some things are just meant to be. She wanted to care for animals. It was the best thing she could ever imagine doing.

Hannah especially loved the family dog Benny, a big, boisterous, loveable golden retriever. It was usual for her to have her breakfast and then take Benny for a quick morning walk. She only walked to the end of the street to visit Mr Fryer, who was always waiting patiently by the gate with a friendly smile for Hannah and a crunchy dog biscuit for Benny. This morning ritual served multiple purposes.

Mr. Fryer, who was now 87, had lost his wife to cancer just ten months ago. They had been married for sixty years, and, for Mr Fryer, it was as though he had lost his right arm when she died. It is so hard to imagine the enormity of that kind of loss when you have shared sixty years of your life with the one person who has always been there, day and night, right by your side only to one day suddenly be gone. The cavernous hole in your life, is all that is left that serves as a constant and continual reminder of all you have lost.

Christine had kept an eye on Mr. Fryer, initially inviting him for meals and taking around casseroles, but, as time went on, she had noticed he had begun to withdraw from the world, staying in his dressing gown for whole days. It was then that Christine decided to start sending Hannah and Benny over for a morning wake-up call. On that first day, after knocking on the door and getting him out of bed, Christine had instructed Hannah to tell Mr. Fryer that tomorrow she would meet him at the gate with Benny, and so a much-loved morning ritual had begun. In truth, this had probably saved his life. Mr. Fryer adored Hannah and Benny, and their daily meetings gave him a reason to get out of bed. Christine was quite pleased with the way this had worked out. Mr. Fryer now had something to look forward to each day, a reason to get up, and Hannah had felt very grown up that she had been given this most important responsibility. Of course, Benny was fairly happy too. For a dog he had hit the jack-pot; a walk *and* a biscuit was gold.

Hannah loved her dog. Well, really it was the family dog, but Hannah considered him to be hers. She brushed him, fed him and walked him. These were her chores, but she never thought of them as chores; she would have done them anyway. She often noticed how happy Benny was when she walked him and it made her feel happy too.

Sniffing, walking and wagging his tail, nothing ever seemed to bother him. Life for dogs seemed so simple. A pat, a smile, a walk is all he needed to be completely joyful, and even at her young age of eight years old, Hannah often thought to herself, '*Yes, I think we could all learn a lot from dogs.*'

Benny was the personification of non-judgemental unconditional love, all wrapped up in a warm, fluffy fur coat. Hannah could see this. Benny had a certain way of putting life into perspective for her.

Mark also loved Benny, but lately he had become less interested in real world family matters as his life continued to move in a new direction.

Hannah felt a little sad this morning that Mr. Fryer would not be waiting at the gate for them today. He had an appointment with his doctor, so Hannah had agreed to walk Benny to see him after school at 4:30 instead.

"It's a date," said Mr Fryer happily.

Hannah was meant to have another brother, but her mother had a miscarriage when she was seven months pregnant, and he died. She had been told it was very sad, and her mother took a long time to get over the loss. Christine was not sure that she ever wanted to have any more children. The whole experience of losing one unborn child and the possibility that it could ever happen again was too much for her to contemplate. This fear resulted in her not even wanting to take the risk.

Hannah had been told she was an *unexpected* surprise. This was fortunate she had often thought. She actually quite liked being an *unexpected* surprise. It was somehow comforting, in some way she felt that this meant that she was destined to be, and of course, Hannah did *love* surprises. She was the youngest by seven years. Her older sister Jessica, now fifteen, was in Year Nine at school. Jessica was moody a lot of the time and never really wanted much to do with Hannah. She often called her a brat and always told her to get out of her room.

* * *

It was 7:05am when Jessica made her way down the stairs that morning. She had a Year Nine Maths exam and wanted to get to school early to cram a little more before the nine o'clock bell rang. Unlike Mark, *this* morning's cram may well be the only study Jessica had done for this particular exam. Maths, or anything else for that matter, did not come easily for her. As she passed by Mark's room, she was aware of an unusual sound, a kind of thud. 'Oh, I wonder what he's dropped,' she thought with a wicked kind of hope that he may be about to get into trouble. *It would be great if he had spilled something on the carpet, or smashed something precious, just so he could get into trouble for once,* she thought. He was always Mr. Perfect and could do no wrong. She could have gone in and caught him out. That would have been fun, an opportunity too good to miss, but she couldn't be bothered today. She had other things on her mind; she had Maths to think about. Let him clean it up himself. *Perfect Mark has made a mistake.* She smiled a slightly nefarious, knowing smile as she continued past his room and on down the stairs.

He *was* perfect Mark; he was always a hard act to follow. All of the teachers used to ask with incredulity, "Jessica Fredrick?"

"Are you Mark Fredrick's sister? *Really?*" As though this were some kind of impossibility, and she must surely be lying.

"Well, who would have thought?"

"You're nothing like your brother."

"Mark...Mark...Mark...."

He was everywhere, the best at everything he did. He was *Captain of the Universe!* It was so unfair to *normal* Jessica who had to follow him through school, but that is how it had always been. Even in kindergarten her teacher constantly reminded her, *"Oh, you're not like your brother, are you?"*

Now, when you are told something over and over from such a young age, constantly compared to an unachievable standard, and always found to be lacking, it has a certain impact. There was certainly a part of her that was well aware that all of this was not actually Mark's fault. In fact, he was the most amazing brother: *of course he was*. He never wanted to be compared to others, he never asked for it to happen, it just *did* happen—a *lot*. Now, don't get me wrong; Jessica loved her brother, but *just once, just one time* it would be nice to see him mess up.

Alex had long since left the house to travel to the airport for a 7:10 flight to Sydney. He was attending a morning meeting that was scheduled for 9:30 in the opulent head office of his legal firm, which overlooked Sydney Harbour. He was now a senior partner in the law firm. These trips were not uncommon although many had now been replaced by the firm's private internet *'group business meeting'* software —but not this one. He and the other senior partners had all been summoned to attend. As he sat in the Qantas business lounge at Tullamarine airport sipping freshly ground coffee, he wondered what the meeting would unveil. Nobody had been told why they had all been summoned, so there had been plenty of speculation but Alex suspected something big was about to be announced. By the time he returned home on the four o'clock flight, something would be different, that was for sure; he wondered what. He turned off his mobile phone, had his last sip of coffee, and got ready to board his plane.

Christine glanced at her watch after pressing the send button on her computer keyboard. The call for agenda items for the midweek meeting was now on its way.

7:20 am. "Damn it Mark! *Where are you?*" she said out loud without thinking. She was about to close down her computer and go upstairs to tell him to hurry up, when Hannah shot past her, Benny in hot pursuit.

"I'll get him, Mum," she said happily as she bounded up the stairs.

"Okay, just tell him to hurry up."

Christine continued to close down the computer as she noticed

Benny sitting at the bottom of the stairs. This was somewhat surprising; Benny was always one step behind Hannah, wherever she went, he followed.

"What's the matter, boy?" she asked as she walked over to him.

Benny was not moving. He looked up at her with sad eyes that expressed more than he could ever say. A hardly audible whine came from him as Christine glanced up the stairs to see Hannah, pale and frozen in a state of shock as she stood in the threshold of Mark's room.

Christine immediately sensed something was horribly wrong and without thinking her maternal instinct sprang into action and she leapt the stairs, three at a time.

"Hannah, what's wrong?" she demanded, panic-stricken. No answer was forthcoming. Hannah stood, motionless. She remained transfixed on what she saw inside Mark's room. Christine got to the top of the stairs and pushed past Hannah, still frozen in the doorway. The scene that confronted her would burn so deeply into her psyche that it would haunt her till her dying day. She let out a blood-curdling scream as she raced to her son, somehow managing to find strength far beyond her own to lift him and awkwardly release the tight noose around his neck, enabling her to lay his lifeless body on the floor.

"*HANNAH!*" she screamed, "Call an ambulance NOW!"

Hannah did not move; she could not move. Sensing Hannah's terrifying shock that had her rooted to the spot, and with no ability to comfort her in any way, Christine screamed even more loudly for her older daughter.

"*JESSICA...JESSICA! I NEED YOU! RIGHT NOW!*"

Jessica appeared at the door and she took in the surreal scene unfolding in her brother's bedroom. The look on her face was one of complete horror and confusion. She stared in disbelief at the loosened noose that still hung, swinging gently from the overhead rafters.

"Don't come in Jessica—" Christine directed.

"Take Hannah down stairs *right now* and call 'ooo' and tell them it's an emergency!"

Jessica did not move; her eyes were affixed to the horror before her.

DO IT—NOW JESSICA!" Christine ordered in a voice that jolted Jessica into action.

Christine then began CPR in a fight against time to save the life of her first-born child.

4

MARK

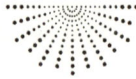

Mark could hear that it was Hannah who was happily running up the stairs to hurry him up that morning. The concern he felt for his little sister and what she was about to witness was something he could not have foreseen. He looked at Grace as if hoping that the inevitable calamity could be avoided, but alas it could not.

"She was not supposed to be here! She was supposed to be up the street with Mr Fryer!" Please, please stop her, please!

We are here to observe only, Mark; we cannot change what is.

As Hannah opened the door to Mark's room her happy smile instantly vanished and it was as though she had been frozen solid in time. She tried to scream, but no sound escaped her. Her mouth hung half open as her eyes remained involuntarily fixed on the gruesome scene before her.

Mark moved toward her and tried to protect her from what she was witnessing, but he was unable to block her view. He was unable to halt the unstoppable events that he himself had put into motion minutes before. Hannah was as unaware of his spiritual presence as she was of everything else at that precise moment, except for one thing, the horrific scene before her eyes of her brother hanging grotesquely before her.

Mark helplessly looked on as his mother pushed her way past Hannah, still motionless in the doorway, as she made her way into his bedroom where she began her valiant effort to save his life. All of this played out in front of him. Time seemed to have no meaning where he was. He could not tell if a few minutes had elapsed or if it had been an hour. It was as if he were watching some kind of crazy movie that *he* was starring in. He was there— but he was not there. Well, his body was there, he could clearly see it, yet *he* was over here, detached from his earthly form and only capable of observing. It was as though his mind was deceiving him with an elaborate confabulation, despite the apparent contradictory evidence, his own body, being glaringly obvious right in front of him. He was dead, well his body was dead, but *he* was certainly not dead.

He spoke to his mother to tell her he was all right; he wanted to let her know his pain was gone. He wanted to tell her he loved her and not to be sad, but she could not hear him.

Christine was lost in her own heroic actions as she frantically attempted to bring her son's body back to life.

Mark had become aware of the ambulance arriving from the direction of Mr. Fryer's house. He could hear the sirens sounding, but astonishingly enough he could also *see* them pulling up out the front. It seemed that he now had an ability to be in all places simply by mere thought alone. Mark pondered this exceptional realisation as he noted yet again, that his newfound unworldly ability did not concern him at all. Everything here, wherever 'here' was, now seemed normal, although *normal* now embraced an expansive new meaning, and even this seemed quite *normal* to him.

He continued to observe the ambulance arrive from this peripheral vantage point, he saw it pull to a stop outside his home, and a male and female paramedic got out of the vehicle with their equipment and rushed to the front door.

Mark had often entertained the idea of being a paramedic, although the thought of some of the things he would witness being out there 'on the front line' made him reconsider his choices. The irony of this thought was now well and truly lost to him as he continued to observe the paramedics' unrushed confident demeanours—their training had taught them well— to be calm in such emergencies. They entered Mark's house and were directed upstairs by Jessica, who had been crying inconsolably as she had tried in vain to call her father. The paramedics quickly evaluated the situation and set to work. A second ambulance soon appeared. Mark noticed that this one was a MICA: a Mobile Intensive Care Ambulance. Having already been briefed on the details of what they were about to encounter, they quickly made their way inside and up the stairs to join their colleagues. Again, Mark wanted to tell them all he was all right, that there was no need to rush, he wasn't even in his body anymore, but again his words could not be heard.

It now seemed there were people everywhere. There were intravenous lines, a defibrillator and heart monitor. Pads and leads of every kind were being put all over his bare chest. Someone was putting a breathing tube into his mouth and attaching a bag and mask connected to oxygen. The heart monitor showed no cardiac activity. The scene was frenetic. CPR was continued, drugs were given, and seconds became minutes as precious time passed while Mark's horrified mother looked on. Then against all odds something began to happen. An irregular beat...suddenly Mark heard someone say 'charging...stand clear' as a jolt of electrical current shot through Mark's lifeless body.

As Mark observed the entire scene of his death, the sudden jolt of pain surged through him, causing him to gasp as he looked on. He was somehow now once again connected to his body. He was very aware of the unpleasant heaviness which had begun to return. Again, someone called out the command to stand clear, and another jolt of electricity once again rushed through Mark's body. An irregular cardiac rhythm was desperately trying to establish itself. It was a fight against time, but had it been too long?

* * *

Alex's flight had landed ahead of time, and it was 8:22am when he found himself comfortably seated in the taxi that was to take him to his head office in Sydney for the much-anticipated meeting. He had been so quick to leave the plane he had not yet turned on his phone. He was considering leaving it off, as he really did not wish to be disturbed this morning with minor distractions. Alex wanted to be completely focused on the impending meeting, and it was only now that he was finally able to take a deep relaxing breath, that he decided against his better judgement to turn it on. When he did, he saw that he had eleven missed calls; eight from his daughter Jessica's phone, two from his mother and one from Christine.

Seconds later his phone rang again. The telephone call that had interrupted his taxi journey was shocking and catastrophic. His son was on his way to hospital in an ambulance after trying to hang himself, was all he had been told by his mother. She had been called in to look after both of his daughters, who were naturally traumatised by the morning's events. Christine had gone ahead in the ambulance with Mark as the paramedics worked to save his son's life. Alex could not make sense of this information.

"*Hanged himself ...?*" *He uttered, disbelievingly.*

"*No...Not Mark...No...what are you saying?* Mark would never..."

"Just get home as soon as you can. *Please!*" his mother cut him off.

"The girls need you, Alex."

Alex immediately instructed the taxi driver to turn the cab around and hurry back to the airport as fast as he could. The driver, having overheard Alex's words, and sensing the urgency in his voice, did not question this. He turned the cab around and headed back to the airport as soon as it was safe to do so. He did not say a word as he dodged and weaved through the Monday morning Sydney traffic as though his own life were on the line.

From the back seat, a pale, shocked Alex Fredrick called the airport on his mobile phone. His frequent business class flights allowed him certain privileges, and he was about to call in some favours.

"I need to get on the next available flight back to Melbourne. It's an emergency!"

He sat in the back of the taxi, tears forming in his eyes as he tried to make sense of what he had just been told, but he could not; it made no sense.

He was booked on the next available flight to Melbourne, which was boarding as his taxi arrived back at the airport drop off area. His Arabian taxi driver jumped out of the car, handed him his briefcase as he shook his hand and said, "No charge my friend. May Allah be with you and your family."

He would have to run. He had a special escort through the security point and ten minutes after arriving at the airport and for the second time that morning, he was boarding his flight. He looked at the mobile phone in his hand and quickly sent a text to his boss. He typed four words and pressed send, before once again turning off his phone and fastening his seat belt for take-off. The time was 8:47am.

* * *

Mark was transported to the hospital accident and emergency department via ambulance. Christine was escorted into a private waiting room. She was not permitted to witness what happened from that moment on; she just had to endure the terrible wait all alone in this cold, unfamiliar place.

How many people had waited here for news of their loved ones, just as she was doing right now? How many of those people waited only to be told the tragic truth that their loved one had not survived? How many had been blessed to have different news? Which would it be for her? She wanted Alex, she needed Alex. He was on his way, but she needed him *now!* He was taking too long. She hadn't spoken to him yet. How would he have taken the news, what would he have thought? He surely could never believe that his eldest son would, *could* ever do such a thing. Yes, perhaps it was an accident.

Oh my God, how has this happened? Why didn't I see this coming, or did I see it coming, was I just too fucking busy to do anything about it? I knew there was something wrong. I felt it, and I didn't make time for it!

How was it possible that her son had been feeling so bad that he actually *intended* to take his own life? How was that even possible? How could it be that she, Christine—*his own mother*—had not known? It must have been an accident, but instinctively she also knew that it was *not* an accident. Had her son been struggling so much that he had deliberately planned and chosen to take his own life, and all the while she had known nothing about it? She had no idea what he must have been going through. How could she have not seen it? She was his mother for Christ's sake. She had failed him miserably.

She looked at her watch on her shaking wrist and hoped that Alex would soon arrive.

* * *

The fight to save Mark's life was exceptional and courageous, but after approximately 85 minutes of cardiopulmonary resuscitation they were unable to re-establish an effective cardiac rhythm, and Mark Fredrick was declared dead at 8:48am on that Monday morning 18th of March.

The Doctor at the hospital came out from the resuscitation area to speak to Christine who stood alone in the private waiting area. The look on his face terrified her.

"I'm so sorry…" the doctor began as Christine let out a primal, guttural scream which interrupted his words, but she had heard enough.

"NOOOOOOOO!" she screamed, as instantaneously she was overcome with a physical pain in her heart, and at the very same time, she felt her legs betraying her. She fell to the floor while everything around her began to spin and blur. She began to dry retch and was about to vomit. A nurse rushed to assist her. She could not think, she could not feel. She was aware that the doctor and the nurse were helping her to a chair, but her body was not her own. She could see the nurse's mouth moving but she heard nothing more. The pounding in her head was deafening. The doctor tried to explain that the amount of time that Mark's body had been without oxygen was just too long, and if he had survived, Mark's heart and brain would have been irreparably damaged, but Christine's panic-stricken mind had shut down and could not process any of it.

* * *

Mark looked on in the waiting room, moment by moment witnessing the disturbing hospital scene before him as his mother continued to endure the worst day of her life, all alone. Why isn't there anyone here with her, he thought? She shouldn't be alone. He wanted to tell her he was sorry; he wanted to comfort her and tell her he loved her. If only he could tell her she *was* a good mother and this wasn't her fault.

He needed her in some way to understand he was all right, although right now he himself did not really understand. He wanted her to know that he was not really dead, and that he felt an overwhelming feeling of love flowing through him, whatever 'Him' was now. It certainly wasn't the lifeless body in the other room that he had, not long ago, stepped away from; yet here he was, still Mark, but not *that* Mark. He had so many questions. As they arose, one by one, he seemed to know the answers. He realised that this place, this reality that he was experiencing, *was* home. Not like the home he knew and lived in with his family; this was a different home. Mark felt that he was being shown all of this, for a reason he was yet to identify.

He turned to look for Grace, and it was almost as though his very thoughts brought her into his awareness; she immediately appeared right beside him. He remembered something about quantum physics and how atoms or electrons—he couldn't remember which—appeared in the observation field when you looked for them, and disappeared from the field when you weren't looking for them. His teacher had said something about the very act of observing altered and influenced what happened to the particles. A bizarre concept, but Mark wondered if this was the same. He wondered if Grace had appeared just because he had thought of her. Regardless, here she was, and it was comforting to see her.

Grace seemed to be able to perceive everything. Mark intuitively felt that she was aware of all things he had been observing, and he was now wondering if *his* act of observation could also alter the outcome. He wondered if it were possible for him to in some way comfort his distressed mother. *Please Mum*, he thought, *don't be so upset, I am fine.* He wanted to hold her and somehow make this better, to let her know he was all right, but he couldn't.

He looked at Grace. "How can I help her? How can I stop her pain? I don't want her to feel this. She doesn't deserve to feel this."

In that moment he truly regretted his choices. Right now, in this peaceful space, it was hard to remember why he had chosen this. Feelings, and even thoughts, were different here.

Grace smiled a heavenly smile, which comforted him as she let him understand once again that he could do nothing to interfere. He was only here now to observe.

She will survive this Mark, is all Grace said.

His gaze returned to his mother. He wasn't so sure.

"I need to see my son—" Christine sobbed.

The nurse gently explained that they would need a few minutes and then she could see him. She asked if there was anybody they could contact for her.

"Is there a Mr. Fredrick?"

Christine suddenly remembered Alex. He would be on his way. What would she tell him? How could either of them make sense of this? How could she tell him she had allowed this to happen on her watch? She was supposed to be looking after him, but she was checking stupid emails!

STUPID FUCKING EMAILS!

She couldn't tell him. She again felt as though she were about to faint, and she must have looked like it too, because the nurse rushed to her side to help her to lower herself safely to the floor. Another nurse placed a pillow gently under her head as Christine's heart pounded and her world began to spin, again.

"Mark" she sobbed. "No, No, NO—this can't be happening."

"This is my fault. I was meant to look after him and I didn't..."

"Alex, I need Alex."

"Don't call him, please don't— he cannot be alone when he hears this."

Then, again: "I need to see him."

Christine tried to sit up, but her head immediately throbbed and spun and she lay flat again.

"Mary Fredrick, your mother-in-law has been calling," said Susan, the young nurse who was now holding Christine's hand, checking her pulse.

"As staff, we can't tell her anything that has happened—would you like to speak to her?"

How does she do this? thought Christine, instinctively wanting to apologise for the trouble she was causing, but then realising how completely idiotic that sounded.

How can these people endure such sadness?

"Oh my God—the girls—how will I tell the girls?" Christine's mind was spinning again, and it now seemed to have a life of its own.

"No, don't tell her anything." Christine could not think of anything in this moment, but the one thing she did know was that she needed to be with her children when they learned this terrible news.

Time had passed; she wasn't sure how long. She was now able to sit up without feeling as if she was going to faint. She had been given a glass of water by the nurses, but they would not let her walk. They said she was in shock and she needed to take things very slowly. Susan had asked her to wait till Alex arrived before she saw Mark. Christine had cried at the thought of this but agreed. It was true, she did feel anxious about seeing her son, however, the image she currently had burned into her memory was not one she cared to think about either.

"Chris?"

Christine turned her head and saw Alex standing in the doorway staring at her. He needed only that one look to know that his worst nightmare had come true. Christine gently shook her head in complete disbelief, as she saw a look of horror appear instantly on her beloved husband's face. She had never seen a look like that before.

Tears streamed from her eyes and continued down her now pale cheeks, leaving discreet, nearly invisible tracks behind that removed what was left of her foundation. It was as though the very sight of him caused every emotion that she had felt in that moment to intensify. Tears and a painful agony overcame her. How was it possible that she could feel any worse? The physical pain in her chest was unlike anything she had ever experienced. She wondered if she were about to have a heart attack, and she really did not care.

Emotion poured out uncontrollably, as if from her very core, like a painful damaging torrent, letting Alex know for sure that his beloved son had not survived. His hand came up to his face, covering his mouth, as he sharply drew in his breath. Almost as if frozen in time, he appeared to stop breathing. He tried to process what was happening. In the space of a few short hours, their entire world had been turned upside down, and it would never be the same again. He moved toward Christine and held her tightly as tears now freely flowed from them both. No words were needed in that moment; a gentle rhythmic movement of their bodies accompanied their sobbing as husband and wife, mother and father, tried to comfort each other amidst the total insanity of this moment. No words or explanations could in any way make sense of this *tragic* nonsensical situation. There would be time for words later, but, for now, Alex and Christine stood in each other's embrace, and steadied themselves for the reality of what was to come.

* * *

It was with the heaviest heart that the school principal, Gregory Preston, found himself sitting in his office with the phone in his hand, ready to convey the terrible news to Monica McKinley on that Monday afternoon. He hesitated before dialling. He was not sure of the words to use to express his deepest regret. He was very aware of the relationship her son Hamish had shared with Mark for the whole of their secondary school experience. He had witnessed the two boys from afar for most of those years as their friendship grew in strength and resilience. Their alliance was based on similar personal qualities and interests, which had served to make them almost inseparable.

His school captain had not arrived on that Monday morning, and nobody, not even Hamish McKinley, had heard from him to explain his absence. It was curious to note that the other Fredrick family student, Jessica, had also been marked absent on the morning roll call.

As was the usual policy, the school receptionist, Maria, called the Fredrick household to establish a reason for the absence.

The phone had only rung once when it was immediately answered by a breathless woman stating that it was 'Mary Fredrick speaking.' the children's grandmother.

Mary had no news to tell the school, but she did say that there had been an accident and Mark and his mother were at the hospital, and Jessica would not be attending school today.

"I'm sorry to hear that," the receptionist had said in a supercilious voice. She then began to launch into some monologue about the importance of the school's absentee policy, but before she could get the words out, Mary abruptly said, "Thank you," and hung up the phone.

Mary, a strong-willed woman, who was in no mood to be polite to a complete stranger today, had thought to herself that *it was none of this woman's bloody business*. She had needed to keep the telephone line free in case there was any news from the hospital.

Mary was the furthest person from a gossip that you could possibly imagine. She had been born at the tail end of WWII and was now in her middle 70s. She had always lived with the unspoken rule that you kept your business to yourself. 'Tell them only what they need to know', she used to say to Alexander when he had been growing up. Now, at this most crucial of moments, until she herself knew what was happening, she was definitely not going to engage in idle speculation with a school receptionist. This was a family matter, and she would, at all costs, protect her family from the hurtful conjecture that always follows an incident such as this.

Her heart was heavy with despair. She adored her grandson and in some way, she felt that she had failed him. She had not been able to protect him from the cruelties of life that had led him to take such dire action, but, to the best of her ability, she would protect him and the rest of the family now.

THE MORNING AFTER THE DAY
BEFORE

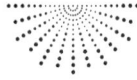

M r. Fryer had waited at the gate at 4:30pm, as arranged with Hannah on that Monday afternoon. She and Benny had not arrived. After a short wait he had gone back inside to prepare a cup of tea. Perhaps he had been mistaken. He would see her tomorrow at their usual time.

On Tuesday the 19th of March, dog biscuit in hand, Douglas Fryer patiently waited once again for Hannah and Benny to arrive for their much-loved morning visit.

He had missed them yesterday, and he had good news to tell Hannah about his previous day. He had discovered a little hidden bookshop. It was home to the most delightful collection of animal colour picture books Mr. Fryer had ever seen. He had taken his time to meticulously survey the collection, after which he had carefully chosen the one that he thought Hannah would love the most. He had developed a deep loving connection to this little girl who he believed. had actually saved his life. She had brought him back from the brink; that much was certain.

Mr. Fryer held tightly to his carefully chosen gift-wrapped book. He currently concealed it in his left hand, behind his back, in order to surprise Hannah when she was due to arrive, but it was getting late. He wondered where they were. He glanced at his watch and he waited patiently. After another ten minutes he slowly turned around and made his way back to his front door. They were never late and Hannah had never before forgotten their meeting. Perhaps she had misunderstood that he would be back today; an uneasy feeling began to stir within him. He had been a high-ranking combat soldier in the Vietnam war in the late 60s and early 70s, and had developed an uncanny instinct that had always served him well. Unlike Hannah, he did *not* like surprises. He would walk down to the Fredricks' house a little later and check that everything was all right.

* * *

The black sky was threatening rain that Tuesday morning, and there was an unseasonable chill in the air. Christine lay on her undisturbed bed, fully clothed, and prayed for sleep. She had not slept all night. She felt as though she was in the middle of the worst possible nightmare. If only she could go to sleep; then perhaps she would wake up and discover that it had all been a terrible, horrendous dream. But she could not sleep, and it was not a dream.

The rain finally began to fall, hitting the window with a gentle rhythmic sound that assured Christine that she was definitely awake and living in her own nightmare. She felt numb; she could not think. It was as if her mind had deserted her body. A fog of confusion had descended upon her and with its presence came the end of any logical thought. There was no logical thought for this situation. This was not logical. This did not make sense. How could her son have taken his own life? How could her only son be dead?

She was a mother; it was who she was.

How could this have happened?

How could she have let this happen?

Her children were more important to her than anything in this world; more important than her stupid job, a job that had taken so much of her time, *more* important than her own life!

Had she put her job in front of her son's needs?

Why didn't she see this coming?

How could she NOT have seen this coming, and how on God's earth could she have let this happen?

Why didn't she know?

These and other repetitive thoughts and so many questions bombarded her mind. The heavy sense of guilt she felt was mercifully, partly alleviated by the complete numbness that enveloped her.

She was unable to think.

None of this made any sense.

Alex lay in the bed beside her; he had fallen asleep only forty minutes before. He was also in his clothes, under the quilt. Neither of them wanted to get into the bed. To do so somehow seemed normal, and this was not a normal day. She stared at his slumbering body wondering if he was dreaming. He was exhausted, emotionally and physically. As she looked on, she felt a stirring of resentment begin in the pit of her stomach. She pondered how it was that he could sleep at all. She wondered if *her* growing guilt would ever allow her to sleep again.

Her mind flashed back to yesterday. It seemed so long ago yet it was only a few short hours, and so much had happened since then. She remembered Alex had held her so tightly as they walked into that room at the hospital, to see their beautiful boy lying there, lifeless and cold; laid out on a gurney beneath a white hospital sheet. The staff had tried to make him look the best they could, but the discolouration around his neck was unmistakable. Christine had gasped again when she saw it, as though it truly confirmed what she had struggled to fully grasp. Her first-born child was dead. He had taken his own life, and there was nothing she could do to change that. Alex had held her tight to stop her collapsing as she had felt her legs weakening again. He too was shocked by the vision in front of him. He had never seen a dead body before, and this was his own son.

Alex stirred, awakened and turned his head to meet her gaze. Her tears said it all, reality quickly filtered back into his awareness almost instantly; he had not been dreaming.

* * *

Hannah and Jessica sat silently in the kitchen as Alex's mother made them toast and hot chocolate. The girls did not feel like eating, but they thanked their Grandma Mary for making it. Jessica took a few small bites to show her appreciation. It was as though the act of making it enabled them all to pretend that somehow everything was still okay, but it wasn't okay. Hannah didn't feel like anything was ever going to be okay again. She slipped her toast off the side of her plate and surreptitiously handed it to Benny sitting by her feet. Benny, who would ordinarily eat anything that came his way, also seemed to understand that something was very wrong this morning because he just sniffed it and turned his head away leaving it untouched.

Hannah was so young; she did not possess the tools to deal with what she had witnessed yesterday. She had hardly spoken a word all day as she sat in stunned silence with her ever present companion Benny by her side. Everyone in the family had been affected by this unspeakable event in their own way. Today they were all in survival mode as they each attempted to understand the catastrophic consequences of this tragedy.

Jessica was beginning to discover her own demons about the order of events and her potential part in the timing of the discovery of this terrible incident. Her head had already begun to fill with so many '*what if*' questions, and the heavy weight of the burden of some of the answers was beginning to cause a new self-loathing to take root.

She inwardly chastised herself for her selfish thoughts of yesterday where she had hoped her brother was finally going to do something bad and get into trouble.

Who thinks such things? she silently berated herself.

The feelings she had around this were silenced by her guilt.

She could not tell anyone what she had wished. She felt wicked.

She could not tell anyone that she had walked past her brother's room at the very moment of his suicide and she could have prevented it...*if only* she had gone in, *if only* she had not been so vile, *if only* she had been a good sister, *if only* she was a good person; Mark would still be alive.

How could she tell her mother that this was all her fault?

How could she ever forgive herself?

She stared at the toast on her plate and excused herself from the table. She went upstairs to vomit the small morsel of toast she had eaten. She did not deserve to eat. She did not deserve to live. She was a disgusting person. She avoided looking at herself in the mirror as she could not stand to see the guilt in her own eyes.

This *was all her fault,* and nothing would ever be the same.

That day was spent just going through the motions. There were tears and there was silence. Nobody really knew what to say and everyone seemed to feel comfortable enough to just sit in the quiet. There were questions; everyone had them, but there were no answers. Jessica had never heard the house so quiet, and Hannah didn't even seem to notice. She just sat and stroked Benny.

All the Grandparents arrived. Grandpa Bob and Grandma Mary, Alex's parents, and Christine's parents; Nanna and Poppa, aunts and uncles all arrived, bringing casseroles that nobody wanted to eat and flowers that nobody wanted to see.

"Thank you," Christine said politely as she took them all.

* * *

It was about 4.30pm when Douglas Fryer knocked on the door of the Fredrick's home. There were many cars in the driveway and he could smell the aroma of some sort of lamb casserole cooking. Nanna Rose and Grandma Mary had placed it in the oven to heat up for all of those who might be hungry. They were both well aware that nobody *was* actually hungry, but it gave everyone something else to focus on. Grandpa Bob slowly opened the heavy wooden carved Oak door to find Mr. Fryer standing there, and in that moment Douglas Fryer knew something terrible had happened. Douglas had seen a lot of death in his eighty-seven years and he recognised that look; it was not one he cared to remember.

"Who?" was all he asked.

Tears welled in Bob's eyes as he looked at the ground struggling to find his voice. "It's Mark," he finally said. "He's dead, Doug."

"What! Mark? How?"

The two older gentlemen's eyes met. No words were needed to convey the message that Douglas received loud and clear. Mark had taken his own life.

"Oh my God," Douglas gasped and staggered back a step.

"Hannah—how's Hannah, and Jessica?" he asked.

"They are ok. Come in, please," said Grandpa, but Douglas Fryer would not come in.

He had an immediate heavy stabbing pain in his chest and sudden radiating pain down his left arm. He suddenly realised he needed to get home to take his Anginine tablets.

"I won't impose. Please give them my condolences," he said as he turned to walk home.

Douglas sat in his lounge room not knowing if he should call the ambulance; the pain in his chest was subsiding now after a second dose of Anginine. He had never been troubled by significant heart issues in the past, but his tough battle worn heart had been broken ten months ago after the passing of his precious Marguerite. He was so devastated by her death that he had wished he too had died. The pain in his heart since that time had been palpable. He had prayed for death, but death did not take him then and he was bloody well determined that death would not take him now.

Now he was needed. Now he had a purpose. Now he had to be there for the little girl who had been there for him during his darkest days. Hannah, this beautiful little innocent soul, could never understand the malevolence of a world that would condone such vile acts, as somehow acceptable, somehow just an unfortunate and unchangeable part of life. How could she ever understand that her own brother would choose to leave her? What would she make of that? Mark did not love her enough to stay? Or perhaps that it was in some way her fault? It was unconscionable. She needed him now more than ever. She had been there for him, unquestioningly every day, with a smile on her pretty little face that reminded him of all he had to live for. Her presence and persistence had pulled him out of his self-imposed prison of solitude, and this had forged a strong bond between old and young that was seemingly indestructible. Now it was his turn to be there for her.

He checked his watch; it was five minutes after the second dose of his heart medication and the pain had now almost gone, but he would not ignore it. To do so would be foolhardy, and foolhardy was something that Douglas Fryer was definitely not.

He picked up the phone to call the surgery. A young sounding receptionist answered the phone and said that the doctor had finished consulting for the day; he was doing paperwork and couldn't be interrupted by patient enquiries. She quickly followed up by saying that he, Douglas, would need to call back tomorrow.

The Douglas who had held the rank of Brigadier in the Australian Army was in no mood to be brushed off by a receptionist who, it seemed to him, was more interested in finishing up work for the day herself than tending to the potentially serious needs of patients. Slightly annoyed by this seeming insolence, the once familiar tone of authority and command quickly returned to Douglas Fryer's voice, as he assertively insisted that he be put through to the doctor immediately as a matter of urgency; he was in no mood to be palmed off today. After a stunned silence, the receptionist obediently followed Douglas' orders, just as he had expected. He was used to people paying attention to him when he spoke, and this served him well. Moments later he heard the sound of a benevolent voice on the other end of the phone.

"Dr. Black speaking. How can I assist you?"

Gerald Black was an old friend and had been Douglas' family physician for twenty years. After acknowledging his old friend, Douglas succinctly explained the events leading up to his angina attack and the sudden, unexpected and shocking news that had precipitated his chest pain. He discussed the worry and concern he felt for the whole family, but especially little Hannah. The shock of the news had certainly brought on the pain, of this he had no doubt; however two doses of Anginine had left him feeling comfortable once again. Gerald sounded concerned and instructed Douglas to call an ambulance immediately should it happen again overnight, and he said he would make him an appointment for 8:30 am in the morning. He wanted to examine him and do an ECG. Perhaps his medication needed to be reviewed. Douglas agreed to all the instructions. He would call an ambulance should the acute stabbing pain return. He now felt perfectly fine except for the slight residual ache in his chest that he attributed to the heavy sadness he now carried for the whole Fredrick family, but especially for his little friend Hannah.

He got up to make a cup of tea and to dish himself a bowl of soup from the large pot on the stove. He would go to bed early to rest tonight and save his energy for tomorrow. The slight ache in his chest would feel better after a good night's sleep.

Douglas tucked himself into bed, saying a little prayer for Hannah and hoping that his little friend was...well, in reality, he wasn't sure exactly what he hoped she could be on a night like this, but he prayed anyway. Douglas had witnessed so much death and destruction in his life in the form of war atrocities, but this was difficult, even for him to process. Mark was eighteen years of age. He seemed to be happy. He had a loving family. This was not war.

What the hell had gone wrong?

He prayed for Hannah to be as good as she could be, given these terrible circumstances. He checked his bedside table to ensure his phone and Anginine were both in easy reach, and then turned out his light and rolled over to go to sleep.

* * *

It was 9:35am when the ambulance arrived to Douglas Fryer's home on Wednesday 20th of March. He had not arrived for his scheduled 8:30am appointment that morning. After unsuccessfully trying to contact him, and knowing his old friend well enough to be sure there must be something very wrong for him not to attend his appointment as promised, Gerald Black had called an ambulance to meet him at Douglas's home. Gerald knew where Douglas hid his spare key and he led the way in, calling Douglas as he did. There was no reply and the house was cold. Gerald walked into Douglas's bedroom to see his old friend still in bed. His cold arm stretched out toward the bedside table for the Anginine bottle that remained unopened.

* * *

Mark stood in the corner, looking on as Doctor Gerald Black sat down on his good friend's bed with tears in his eyes. He was beginning to understand the immense and completely unintended consequences of his own actions. He had never considered just who else would be affected by his death, and how these effects would ripple out into the world in unexpected ways. How could he? He had been in no emotional state to have such insights, but he was now beginning to get a glimpse. He looked for Grace, and she was again by his side with a loving smile that conveyed that she was here for him. Unlike Mark, Douglas was not still *present* in this room. Mark wondered why.

"He has gone home Mark, he is no longer here," she said without him even having to ask.

"But why?"

"Because it was his time, Mark. He is being cared for now."

"He is with Marguerite and his spiritual family. He is fine."

Yet Mark wondered why *'he'* was still here. Grace did not answer his thoughts this time. Instead she averted her eyes to what was occurring in the bedroom before her, as Gerald reached over to take his friend's icy hand.

"I am so very sorry my dear old friend," he said.

"You reached out to me and I truly failed you, and for that I will never forgive myself."

He sat for a while trying desperately to reconcile the events of the past 24 hours. How could he have allowed this to happen? He finally stood and looked at the two paramedics waiting patiently behind him. "He has no family left," Dr. Black gestured to them. "Please take him to the hospital, there will need to be an autopsy. I'll call the funeral home and make the arrangements myself. *I'll* be organising the funeral." He turned one last time to look at Douglas as he said, "I'm sorry my friend, I'll make sure Hannah is all right."

As he walked up the corridor, he spotted on the table the carefully wrapped gift that was addressed as follows:

Dear Hannah,

I hope you enjoy this surprise.

With love,

Mr. Fryer x

Reluctantly, Doctor Gerald Black knocked on the heavy carved oak door, that his good friend Douglas Fryer had knocked on not 24 hours before. He waited patiently until it opened. Christine Fredrick stood in the doorway. Her face appeared puffy from crying and lack of sleep, and her hair had not been brushed. She looked exhausted.

"Doctor Black?"

"Mrs. Fredrick, I am so sorry for your loss—"

"Thank you," she said, just going through the perfunctory motions of civilised conversation. She stood there not knowing what to say.

"Come in," she eventually said.

"No thank you, Mrs. Fredrick, I don't want to disturb you at this time. I just wanted to pass on my condolences."

Alex joined Christine at the door to see what was keeping her.

"Doctor?" he said with a concerned, somewhat curious tone of voice.

"Hello, Alex, I am so terribly sorry for your loss. Please accept my deepest condolences."

"Thank you, Doctor Black," Alex nodded.

"I would never want to disturb you at this time, but I'm afraid I have some sad news of my own that I think you ought to know."

Christine turned to Alex, her look expressed confusion—how could there be any sadder news? They both returned their gaze to the Doctor.

"I am so sorry to tell you this, but Douglas Fryer passed away last night."

Christine gasped in disbelief; her hand automatically rose up and covered her mouth.

"No!" she gasped. "You must be wrong, he was here just last night. Dad spoke to him and told him about Mark. He was upset and worried about Hannah!"

Christine gasped again as the immediate implications of that statement rocked her to her very core.

"Oh my God...No—" she almost whispered, as the significance of the situation began to filter through to all present.

"I am very sorry to add to your distress, but I just thought you should know. Hannah will be very upset and it will need to be handled with discretion. This I will leave in your capable hands."

He handed them the gift.

"I found this on his table. He would have wanted Hannah to have it."

"I will be arranging the funeral and I will let you know the details. Please give your whole family my condolences," he said and with a heavy heart. So weighed down by his own guilt and sadness, Gerald Black turned and walked away.

The post-mortem later declared that Brigadier Douglas Fryer died instantly of a massive myocardial infarction, somewhere between 1 am and 4 am, on Wednesday 20th March. The insult to his heart muscle was so severe that death was immediate.

6

THE RIPPLE BECOMES A TSUNAMI

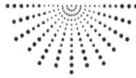

Tuesday 26th March was a cold dark day. The clouds had gathered, looming dark in the sky, and rain was threatening. The wind blew strong that day as if to blow away the sadness, but it could not. The family and friends of Mark Fredrick had come together to celebrate the young life of a beloved son, brother, cousin, friend, fellow student, school captain, employee, athlete and sportsman.

Mark had been all of these things and much, much more.

He was the boy down the street, the ever so friendly supermarket deli attendant, the straight 'A' student; every teacher's dream, and all-round good guy.

So, why were they all gathered here?

Why had this happened?

What had gone wrong?

Where were the red flags that were supposed to protect young boys like Mark?

Was it society that had failed him, or had they?

Had the people who had gathered there that day, in some way failed him?

Every person assembled here was now challenged to answer these questions for themselves, and, even worse, many were left in guilt to wonder why none of them had seen it coming. No one was more perplexed than Christopher Oaks. He stood at the back of the chapel desperately trying to be invisible as he attempted to come to terms with his part in the death of Mark Fredrick.

Christopher had always considered Mark to be like a son. He had taken Mark under his wing and into his high-performance squad of elite athletes after he had first discovered Mark's natural talent shining brightly at a little athletics state championship a little over eight years ago. Even at the tender age of ten, Mark's talent and future potential was unmistakable. He consistently blitzed the field in nearly every track event from sprints to the 1500 metre distance. It was exciting for Christopher to watch, and he knew he needed to help this young boy reach his full potential. Mark had seldom disappointed him. Yes, he had driven him hard—that was true—but Mark had always taken it in his stride, or so it appeared. He had seemed to thrive on the challenges. He had a natural talent that would have taken him far.

Christopher had his eyes set on Tokyo 2020 for Mark. They had discussed it on several occasions and Mark was on track for being ready. March in Australia was championship season. Mark had performed as expected at the state championships in late February. He had already qualified in all his favourite events; all he needed to do was show up on the day at the state championships and his place was assured, but just showing up on the day was not in Mark Fredrick's nature. He was an *'all or nothing'* kind of boy, and even with the additional school requirements of Year Twelve and being school captain, he had still managed to achieve gold in the 100m and 200m sprints, silver in the 400m and just for fun he was awarded a bronze in the long jump, only a few days ago. What had happened between the absolute dizzying heights of that weekend, and the immense and debilitating lows that had contributed to Mark taking the action he did?

The responsibility for not noticing what was going on, for not being aware of those things that were not immediately obvious, was something that would haunt Coach Oaks for the rest of his days. One of his best athletes had not only crumpled under the burden of life's pressures, but his situation had silently spiralled uncontrollably to the lowest point possible, resulting in this tragic outcome. The only option Mark could see for some relief from his pain was this: *How terrible he must have felt, how alone in that moment, how debilitatingly alone—and how was it that he, 'the great Coach Oaks,' could not see what was clearly before him?*

Mark was to compete in four events at the upcoming National Championships in Sydney, Australia in April. With the Olympics a little over twelve months away, there would be coaches and members from Athletics Australia on the lookout for exceptional athletes like Mark. He certainly had the talent to go all the way, he had the determination and he had the drive, but what the hell had gone wrong, and was he, Christopher Oaks responsible? Did he drive this young boy too hard? Would Mark Fredrick still be alive, if not for his beloved coach?

A tear escaped him, and burned his already hot face. He wiped it away with the cuff of his Athletics Victoria navy blue officials blazer. Generally worn with the utmost pride, for the first time ever today, he was not proud to be wearing it. The usual comfortable fit was today irritating him terribly. He tugged at the navy cotton neck tie he wore, and scratched at the collar of his blazer as it itched his neck. It was no mistake that he stood at the rear of the chapel, just out of the sight of Mark's family, almost afraid that everyone present knew what he himself knew; they were all here because someone who was supposed to care and support Mark, had inadvertently added to his overwhelming pressures, and 'that' someone was him.

They were here because he, 'Coach Oaks' had wanted glory, but at what cost?

Were they here because he wanted glory for Mark Fredrick?

Or, were they here because he wanted glory for himself?

Why had he been so stupid?

Why had he been so blind?

As soon as the service was over, Coach Oaks moved quietly in the direction of the side exit. He was travelling against the current of mourners who were moving en masse in the direction of the back of the church. In his attempts to deliberately avoid the rapidly gathering crowd quickly assembling at the entrance of the church, he glanced in the direction of the Fredrick family. He saw Christine and Alex arm in arm shepherding the girls toward the exit. In that moment his eyes met those of Christine Fredrick; he could not quite discern the meaning of the look in her eyes, but he feared that she knew the terrible truth. He immediately averted his eyes and made his way out toward his car, which he had positioned for the discreet exit he knew he would be required to make.

There were over a thousand people who had gathered and who were now all tasked with not only coming together on this extremely sombre day to celebrate Mark's short life, but more importantly to somehow make sense of something that made no sense.

Mark was loved by all present, and they were all present as a testament to that love. It is hard to imagine just how many people's paths we cross in one short life span, but everyone who had gathered had been touched by Mark Fredrick in some way. So many people had come together on this day; some known, some unknown, but all in some way affected by his passing.

His school and fellow V.C.E. students, who were just commencing their most important final year of school studies, were here united as one to show their support and love for someone they truly respected.

Other students from other year levels, who had been elected to represent their school alongside their captain Mark, had flatly refused to go to school today. They had en masse chosen to boycott school, in favour of coming together on this dreadful day to show a sign of solidarity for their former captain; to be there for his family, by not only showing support to them, but also to be there for anyone else struggling with mental health issues on this very sad and difficult day. They intended to send a clear and strong message that this must never happen again. The students were steadfast in their cause.

The wave of support for Mark Fredrick and his family on that day, was nothing short of a tsunami. It was blatantly obvious that Mark had made a massive impact on all he had met during his short life. He had touched the hearts of these people and helped to create so many treasured memories of happier times which none of them would soon forget. Nowhere was this more obvious than at Mark's own school. The school, in an unparalleled move, had no other choice than to declare, as a sign of respect, that all classes would be cancelled to allow any staff and students who wanted to take part in Mark's funeral the opportunity to do so by forming part of a guard of honour to show a united sign of their respect. The end result of this was something to behold.

There were some 140 Year Twelve students who flanked the path from the chapel to the crematorium, forming part of the guard of honour that day, as Mark's coffin was driven away. In an unprecedented show of solidarity never before seen at the school, *every* Year Twelve student and *every* Year Twelve teacher was in attendance. Alongside them was at least 700 other students and teachers not only from Mark's school, but also neighbouring schools. Joining them was another 150 athletes, coaches and participants that had come from Mark's Victorian Athletics association and football association. Side by side in unity over 1000 individuals were all there for one purpose and one purpose only, to stand together to honour an amazing young man, a beloved friend, a fellow student and a talented fellow athlete.

Each person lining the street that day, as Mark's Coffin was driven away, stood in respectful silence, head lowered and all wearing a very visible lime green ribbon representing Mental Health Awareness. For all looking on it was a truly memorable sight. A very clear message was being expressed. These students would not accept any more teenage suicides. This had to stop. This was an issue that had been hidden away, spoken about in hushed tones behind closed doors for far too long. Enough was enough. This subject needed to be brought out into the light and these students would lead the way. This was an urgent matter that needed to be addressed because even one teenage death by suicide was one too many.

After the service, which had lasted almost an hour, Christine and Alex again stood together united in their grief on this most devastating of days. Arm in arm as they walked out of the church and into a life without Mark. Christine looked up and met the eyes of Mark's beloved coach. Coach Oaks had come today as she knew he would; Mark had loved him dearly. Their eyes locked for a mere moment and her expression was blank–she had lost the capacity to be courteous or appropriate and she really did not know what to say to this man. She knew he would be hurting from his own immense loss and again she felt the sharp pangs of her own guilt penetrate the thick, heavy fog of her grief. She quickly looked away as she walked out to the gathering group of mourners.

They spoke the necessary pleasantries to anyone who approached, but they both just wanted everyone to leave. They did not want to stand at the wake with these people and discuss their wonderful son and all the happy memories. Mark was dead, did they not understand that? What else was there to say? He was DEAD!

Finally, after as much as she could endure, Christine felt she could not take anymore. The last week had robbed her of every ounce of energy she had. It had taken her every last effort even to get dressed today, let alone make it through the funeral service, and now she was totally exhausted. There was nothing left for her to give. She had been prescribed a sedative by her doctor, and it was time to take it. She wanted this day to be over. She was aware that her girls needed her, now more than ever, but she had nothing to give them in this moment. Her world was falling apart and it was best she did not take them down with her. She asked her mother to look after them, as she made her apologies and quietly slipped out the back door to return home to the seclusion and solitude of her bedroom.

* * *

Jessica noted her mother's discreet departure. She was also acutely aware that her mother had not said goodbye to her. Jessica's heart sank as she watched Christine disappear silently out the back way. She knew her mother was heartbroken due to the loss of another child, but Jessica's own heart was equally broken, so weighed down with guilt and despair she felt as though she could hardly breathe. She wondered if her mother in some way knew the terrible truth that she, Jessica, was to blame.

Jessica knew *she* was culpable. She could have saved Mark if only she had chosen to go in to his room that morning, to actually open the door and go in and investigate that unusual sound, just as any *responsible* person would have done. If only she had not been so self-absorbed, she would not have chosen to walk right past Mark's room that morning, actually hoping as she did that Mark was finally about to get into trouble. Well Mark certainly *was* about to get into trouble. Trouble of an unequalled magnitude that was now irreversible. Trouble that she could have prevented, if only she were not such a hideous person.

As she watched her mother disappear, she reflected on her mother's actions. She wondered again if her mother did know the truth and hated Jessica for it. She had not been able to look Jessica in the eye since that terrible day, and now this. The thought that her mother somehow knew the unforgivable truth was almost too much for Jessica to bear, and it made her feel physically sick. Not for the first time today, Jessica's mind drifted to what would have been happening behind that closed door on that fateful morning.

Was Mark sorry he stepped off the stool?

Had he actually timed it so he could be saved?

Did he want her to discover him?

Did he regret doing it, and was he praying Jessica would come in to save him?

What would he have thought if he was still conscious and heard her walk away?

Did he hear her there and think, 'Thank God, Jessica will save me?'

These repetitive and continuous thoughts and other equally disturbing ones had plagued her for the last week. It was as though she now had no control of her own mind. These were the last thoughts she had when she finally went to sleep at night, although sleep was not coming easily to her this last week, and these were the very first thoughts that greeted her as her eyes opened in the morning. For Jessica there was to be no respite from the truth. Images also plagued her. The image of Mark's lifeless body on the floor as her mother frantically tried to save him, was one she could not forget. Her mother was a hero: of that she had no doubt. She was valiant in her relentless attempt to save her son. She did not deserve to lose another child; it was not fair. In that moment as Jessica watched her mother leave without a glance, without a word, Jessica wished that it could have been her that died that day, not Mark, as her own self-loathing reached a new low point. She truly believed that everyone would be better off without her.

* * *

Christine found the bottle of prescription medications. As she held them in her hand, she thought of just how easy it would be to take them all and put an end to this horrific pain. Her pain was palpable, not just emotional, but actually physical. She felt it in every cell in her body and it was getting worse as the days went by, not better. She yearned for it all to end and for life to return to normal, but she knew that life would never be normal again. She stared at the bottle for just a little too long, lost in thought. Yes, it would be so easy, but she could *never* do that to her children.

In that moment she gained such insight into just how a person could reach the most devastating low point in their life and actually consider suicide as an option; when life had become too difficult to bear and when there truly seemed like there was no other viable way out. Tears welled in her eyes just when she thought she had none left. Her own son had reached that point. Her own son had felt this bad, and, even worse than this, he had endured his pain alone. He had felt there was no other choice, and this realisation devastated her.

Christine opened the bottle and took out one tablet which she washed down with a rather large glass of red wine. She didn't regularly drink, and she certainly *never* mixed medications with alcohol, but today she did not care. It was so wrong but, in that moment, it somehow felt so right. She didn't know what she was supposed to do when she woke up. She had no idea of how life would, or even could, go on normally without Mark.

She pulled back the covers on her bed and slipped underneath, dragging them up over her head as she did. She hoped against hope that mercifully she would somehow just pass out and sleep for a month. She had not slept at all for the past week, as her own demons had plagued her. She was no closer to understanding why this had happened, and what had led Mark to feel that life was not worth living. She was also no closer to forgiving herself for the fact that this *had* happened.

She had known that there *was something* that had been disturbing Mark and she had not taken the time out of her busy schedule to investigate what that '*something*' was. She had made other things a priority and now he was dead. The thought, the word, sent a shudder through her body. Her beautiful boy was *dead*. That was never supposed to happen, a parent should never outlive their children.

She was plagued with memories and feelings of losing her third child by a late pregnancy miscarriage. It had taken her so long to overcome the complete devastation of that, but this was different. This was somehow worse for her, although she never would have believed that was even possible. This was her son that she had carried within her own body for 9 months, and whom she had nurtured and protected for 18 years. She had lived the ups and downs of daily life by his side, the highs and the lows, *and Mark had so many highs*. Why had she been so blinded to the massive lows he must have been enduring all alone?

She held herself responsible for not being able to protect her own son in his own home, the one place he should have been safe. She wondered if she could ever forgive herself for that. She had believed he was safe from the world at home, but it was within the privacy of his own bedroom that the world came crashing in on him.

As she thought about this, she sensed an overwhelming feeling that she was a complete failure as a mother. Not only had she failed Mark, but she had failed the girls. She had failed to protect her girls from such devastation; the loss of a brother and the horror of witnessing what they both witnessed. She was so guilt-ridden about what her beautiful girls had endured that day, she feared it had scarred them both to the point neither of them would ever be the same again. She could now not even look them in the eyes for fear of seeing the havoc that this had caused them reflected back at her. She hated herself for letting this happen. If only she had been a better mother, if only she had been more aware, but she had been so caught up in her stupid work and her trivial meetings that she lost sight of what was really important.

Naturally, the girls had not been to school all week, they had both struggled to come to terms with this tragedy and the sequence of events that had led up to it. There was a part of her that wondered if they also blamed her. Her guilt was a heavy burden for her to carry and it seemed to be getting heavier with each passing day. What *is* a mother's job, if not to protect her children? *She had failed them all.*

* * *

Jessica found Hannah and she took solace in the comfort of just holding her hand. The funeral guests began to file out of the reception area, passing them by, one by one, with such sad looks of pity and compassion on their faces. She heard the near silent whispers of some well-meaning people as they passed, saying statements in such sad voices like; "Poor little things," and, "It's so sad," or "Oh, how terrible for those girls." Jessica tried to shield her little sister from it all. She had been through enough. Hannah hadn't spoken much since the shock of seeing her older brother in his room a little over a week ago; a sight no eight-year-old should ever see. Jessica reflected with guilt: she knew it was a sight that Hannah would *never* have seen at all if only she had opened that door on that fateful morning.

If all of this was not bad enough, on Friday their parents felt they had no other choice but to tell the girls the sad news of the passing of Mr. Fryer two days before. When Jessica heard the news, she wondered if this week could get any worse. All eyes went toward Hannah as she let out a very loud scream.

"*NO! He is NOT dead!*" Hannah had yelled with such conviction. It was almost as though she thought if she yelled it loudly enough and believed it hard enough it would be true. Hannah had jumped to her feet and stared at her parents challenging them on this point. "I don't believe you!" she had said.

Christine, with tears in her eyes, had looked at Alex and wondered to herself just how much her younger daughter could endure.

"I'm so sorry," her father had said to her.

He had held out the gift-wrapped book that Mr. Fryer had wanted her to have.

"He bought this for you, Hannah. He wanted you to have it. It was meant to be a surprise. He knew how much you loved surprises." Alex had spoken with such compassion in his voice and pain in his heart for his younger daughter who surely was about to break down and cry, but Hannah did not cry. She was angry.

Hannah snatched the gift from her father's hands and threw it to the floor, stomping on it as she did.

"You're lying."

"You are a BIG FAT LIAR!"

"I HATE YOU!"

"I don't want that stupid surprise. *I don't like surprises*—I hate them! I HATE SURPRISES!"

Hannah had then run up the stairs to her bedroom and slammed the door with such ferocity that the house shook. She threw herself onto her bed, the impact of which took her breath away. In that moment as Hannah's world seemed to spiral out of control, the escape of air from her lungs as her body impacted with the mattress seemed to cause something to break within her emotionally. As she lay on her bed, tears in her eyes, she had spotted Pabby, her previously discarded teddy bear, on the shelf above her bed where it had laid untouched for over two years. She had told her mother that she was too big for teddies, but Christine did not have the heart to get rid of it; to do so would have meant her little girl was growing up. It was the teddy her Grandmother Rose had given Hannah the day she was born. When Hannah could speak she had called him Pabby. In her childlike babble, Hannah could not pronounce teddy, so Pabby it was to be. For the first time in over two years Hannah had reached up and pulled Pabby down from the shelf and hugged him tightly to her chest as another silent tear escaped her. In that moment Hannah fell silent. With Pabby firmly grasped to her chest, Hannah retreated from this painful world emotionally, and instantly words simply left her.

* * *

The funeral was drawing to its excruciating end.

Jessica held tightly to Hannah's hand, she looked into her little sister's face, feeling a surge of responsibility and guilt for all that had happened. She turned to her little sister and said, "I'm so very sorry Hannah, this isn't fair."

"Come on let's go and find Nanna, I want to go home."

Hannah turned silently and she walked beside her sister, hand in hand, but her face was expressionless.

7

THE UNSEEN CASUALTIES

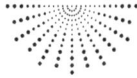

Coach Oaks picked up his mobile phone and sent out a group text to all his athletes.

"No training today."

He had never before cancelled a session this close to the Nationals.

He knew if his athletes wanted to train today, they could run their session without him.

The boys and girls in Mark's squad stared at the unexpected words that had appeared on their phones. Most had already gathered at the track. They glanced at each other, and they all understood the greater implications of this text. There was a moment of silence when nobody knew what to say. One of the older girls, already silently struggling with the loss of Mark Fredrick, began to cry. Two other girls moved into a small huddle and embraced her. Moments later the boys leaned in. The small group of close friends all hugged in silence.

From across the oval, parents looked on. No words were needed, everyone understood. There was not a person here that had not been affected by the events of the last week in some way.

"I'm training," said one of the boys.

"Me too," said another.

"Let's do this for Coach Oaks."

"Yes!" They all agreed.

"I'm doing it for Mark," said the girl who had been crying.

"Let's all aim for PBs at Nationals, for Mark," said another boy.

It was essential for them to just keep running. It's what they did; it was their way to keep focused on something else, on something positive. It was their way to survive this horror and in their own way honour Mark.

This year at the Australian National Athletics Championships they would all be running for Mark. Each and every one of them had all been affected by this tragedy, and not just the athletes, but the athletes' families and the entire athletic community. Everyone knew, and had liked, Mark.

The athletics community was tight knit. Mums and dads who travel great distances to assure their children get to training up to five times a week, and those who travel to competitions all over the state, and all over the country, were affected by this too. To compete at this level requires a massive commitment from not only the athletes, but family members also. All of these athletes, boys and girls, all of their families, their siblings, their siblings' friends, and everyone connected to these people in almost every way imaginable have all been touched by this single event in ways that were seen and unseen. The seemingly endless ripples that continued to flow out in every direction, like an unstoppable pandemic of epic proportions, are immeasurable. Mark's ripples were permeating out at every level of connection, in a relentless and undiscerning fashion such that nobody was spared.

* * *

Hamish McKinley sat on his bed noticing a heavy feeling in his chest, and a knot, tight and unrelenting, in the pit of his stomach. It was Wednesday morning, the day after Mark's funeral, and he was in no mood to go to school today. His mother had called him several times to no avail. He could not even get up the motivation to get dressed. Mark's death had hit him hard. It was as though he was *still* reeling from a massive, violent blow that had completely rocked him to the core, a blow that he never saw coming.

He vividly replayed over and over, the memory of the terrible moment he heard the devastating news that his best friend was dead. The words spoken by his mother in the most compassionate of tones, will forever haunt him. Lying in his bed in his room, the painful memory played once again as though it had a life of its own, one he was unable to control.

"Hamish, I have some *very* disturbing news to tell you, and it's going to come as a shock," his mother had gently said to him.

"I don't know how else to tell you this, so I'll just say it. I'm so very sorry Hamish, it's Mark."

She had taken his hands in hers, as she said with the most heartfelt compassion she could muster.

"Darling, Mark is dead."

Silence had filled the room as Hamish stared at his mother. He had been unable to comprehend what had just been said, it was as though she were speaking a foreign language that he did not understand.

"*W..what?*" he stammered. "What did you just say?"

A shocked expression of bewilderment and confusion had instantly spread across his face.

"He's dead my darling. I'm so sorry." She paused. Tears had filled her eyes. She had not been sure how much to tell her son about the details of Mark's death, but she also knew he needed to know the truth.

She had braced herself before continuing to speak the words her son would never forget.

"He killed himself, Hamish."

"This morning," his mother added gently as she looked into the totally horror-stricken eyes of her son.

Hamish, for the rest of his life, would never be able to forget those three pivotal words. "He killed himself."

His best friend had killed himself!

The panic and disbelief that had flooded through his entire being in that instant, had sent a shockwave through his body unlike anything he had ever experienced before. He could not believe it. Surely this must have been some kind of sick joke, he had thought, but he knew his mother would never do that. His head had reeled in disbelief and confusion as a mix of jumbled words and thoughts bombarded his consciousness.

"NO" he had said out loud. "It can't be true!"

"It's not true. Mum you're kidding me, and it's not funny!" he had said.

But the look on her face had told him she was not kidding.

"It's a mistake. It's got to be. It's Mark! He can't be dead!

No, He's alive. I saw he was in the chat room last night. He has to be alive!

Hamish had begun to cry. Tears had fallen down his cheeks as a physical pain had seemed to radiate out from his stomach and heart simultaneously.

"Mark would NEVER do that!"

"He's my best friend, I know he would NEVER. No, you're wrong. You have to be wrong. Why would you say this? Do you think this is funny? It's not funny! Mum...tell me you are joking...please Mum!"

He really had no idea what had been said after those initial shocking words, but the realisation of what he absolutely knew beyond doubt to be true, was that his mother would *never* have lied about such a thing. He had looked into his mother's eyes and observed the look of pained acquiescence on her face, which had absolutely confirmed what he did not want to believe. It had left him with little doubt, but perhaps she was wrong, he had thought. It was possible. People were sometimes wrong. Amidst all the confusion Hamish had confronted his mother in an angry tone.

"Who told you this rubbish?" he had challenged her.

"Mr. Preston called, Hamish." She had replied with the greatest sadness.

"He wanted you to know before you heard it from someone else."

Instantly upon hearing these words a secondary invisible blow to the gut had winded him again. He had desperately hoped that this was a mistake, although he was soon to come to the brutal realisation that this *was no* mistake. His companion throughout his entire school life and his best friend *was* dead, and Hamish had no idea why.

News such as this can be so shocking that the details and emotions of these moments are never forgotten. They can often be perfectly preserved and imprinted in our subconscious mind just beneath the level of surface awareness, such that they have a lasting negative effect on the recipient, as Hamish was later to discover.

Hamish dragged his thoughts back from the painfully distressing recent past and returned his attention to the present moment. He took a few deep breaths as he sat motionless on his bed.

Over the last week he had continued to have flashbacks of the exact moment he was told the horrific news that his best friend was dead. The word "*dead*" had hit him like a blow to the stomach that had winded him and taken his breath away, leaving him feeling like he couldn't breathe. Every time he remembered that terrible moment, he again felt the horror as though it were still happening, but now the memory was accompanied by the most extreme feelings of anxiety and fear right in the pit of his stomach and in his chest. He did not understand what was happening to him, so he tried not to think about it.

He tried *not* to remember the coffin that was carried out by Mark's crying father, grandfathers, uncles and a cousin, who was only 18 years old, to the waiting hearse. He tried *not* to remember the over-whelming look of sadness on all of their faces. He tried *not* to remember what he felt as he thought of his best friend's cold dead body in that box, and he tried *not* to remember the sound that could only have been Mark's body moving within the coffin as they lowered it to place it in the hearse. He tried *not* to remember his feeling of horror as he feared they may drop the coffin and it might open up revealing the pale lifeless face of his *dead* friend. Most of all, he tried *not* to remember the very last thing he had said to his best friend that would now haunt him till his dying day, filling him with the deepest regret.

If only he had known how Mark had been feeling.

If only he had recognised Mark's struggles.

If only they had not had that fight.

If only he had been a 'good' mate, perhaps Mark would still be alive.

* * *

Monica knocked on the bedroom door again.

"Hamish, you are going to be late and you have a SAC assessment today, she said sensitively. She was very aware that her son had been rocked by the news of his best friend's death. She knew that going to school was the very last thing he wanted to do, but a week had passed, and she hoped that perhaps getting back to some kind of normalcy would be good for him.

Mark Fredrick had been like a member of the McKinley family. The boys had grown up together over the primary and secondary school years. They were inseparable at times, but she had noticed Mark had not been around much lately. She had asked Hamish if there was anything wrong, but he just shrugged it off as nothing serious, just a falling out. They had had fights before, and no doubt they would have them again, she had thought.

Monica, and her entire family were now also grieving the loss of a boy with so much potential, a boy with so much to live for, who had been a part of their family for the last 12 years. A boy she considered to be a second son. It was hard for her to now carry on as normal, because she suspected life would never be quite the same again. It was difficult for her to ask her own son to get up one day after the funeral of his best friend and carry on as if everything were okay, but that's exactly what she found herself doing as she knocked for the third time on the door.

Sitting on his bed, Hamish was well aware he had a SAC scheduled today, but he did not care. He had already decided that he would not be going to school today. The School Assessed Course work, or SACs as they were called by most, were a form of internal school assessment that went toward the end of year results. They were very important to the overall final marks, and previously Hamish would never have considered missing one. His priorities however had now shifted dramatically. He didn't care about school today; in fact, he was unsure if he would ever care about school again in the same way that he had.

Everything had changed for him. He was beginning to realise that life could turn around in a split second and knock you flat, and that was a scary realisation. The ongoing and continuous feeling in the pit of his stomach, which felt like a tight knot that wouldn't unravel, and the associated racing of his heart whenever he thought of his friend's torment, was at times overpowering him. He had never experienced feelings like this before, but he had also never known anyone who had died before.

He would tell his mother he was unwell. To be honest, he did feel unwell. He wasn't sure what was happening to him, he had not been sleeping properly. He just could not stop the unsettling thoughts that were intruding upon his every moment, and the upsetting images that were burned into his psyche that he just could not stop seeing. He imagined his friend's last moments, and his lifeless body hanging from a noose, face blue and eyes bulging, but more than that, he imagined his last moments as he waited for death to arrive. He tried not to think about all the horror of what must have gone on in his friend's room that day, but his mind now had a life of its own. The relentlessness of these thoughts were weighing him down such that he felt he could no longer function. Yes, he decided he *was* unwell. He needed time to sleep but sleep was also becoming a less and less achievable goal.

His mother finally entered his room to find him still in his pyjamas sitting on the side of the bed. He looked terrible.

"Are you sick, love?" She asked.

"Yes, I really don't feel well Mum," he said, half believing he must be coming down with something. He then began to cry. Hamish was not a boy who cried easily.

His concerned mother sat on the bed and just held him.

"I'm so sorry my darling," she said with tears in her eyes. "I just want to wrap you up and protect you, but I can't. It hurts me so much to see you so sad. We will get through this together, Hamish, we really will."

She was worried that Hamish may in some way blame himself for the fact that he had not spoken to Mark for a few weeks, and she needed to reassure him.

"This is nobody's fault Hamish. You know that, don't you?"

Hamish looked into his mother's eyes. He was not so sure.

"Lie down darling," she said closing the blinds and pulling the covers over him. "I'll call the school and explain."

The SAC assessments were so important to the school assessment process that a doctor's certificate was required for any student who missed one. This was quite an inconvenience to many families, but it was one way to ensure that the Year Twelve students were legitimately sick, and not just attempting to get more study time for an examination they were not ready for. "I'll call the GP and arrange for a certificate for you," she said.

Hamish rolled over and faced the wall. He prayed for sleep, but sleep was a luxury he was not to experience today.

His mind went straight to that last conversation he had had with his friend.

It had been heated; it had been senseless. He couldn't remember exactly what had started it, but it had been over, of all things, social media. How foolish he had been to ever let that come between them. Their relationship was built on far more than that, yet he had been stubborn and he had been stupid. He had wanted—no, *needed*—to make a point. *Well what was the point now?* Now his friend was no longer here to voice any opinion. What was the point, that had once seemed so important, worth now? His friend's last words to him were, "*Fuck off and leave me alone!*" His reply; "*Yeah no worries mate. I will fuck off then, I don't need this shit.*" He had turned and walked away from his best friend and stubbornly refused to speak to him again until Mark came to him and apologised. Those words were now echoing in his head and they were threatening to deafen him.

"Fuck off and leave me alone!" Why had Hamish done exactly that? He *had* fucked off and left his friend all alone without the support of his best mate—right at the time he had needed him the most.

"Well who's talking now, you stupid bastard?" Hamish inwardly chastised himself. Mark had put an end to all future conversations. The last word had been spoken. *Full stop. Nothing more to fucking say!*

Hamish had not been there for his friend and for this he would never be able to forgive himself. In his mind he went over and over the last weeks that led up to the death of his best friend. *Why had he been so stubborn? Why had they both been so bloody idiotic?*

* * *

Over the Christmas holidays, Mark had been becoming more and more distant from his friends, and more and more consumed by social media. His sporting activities were suffering as he was actively choosing to spend his time shut away in his bedroom. Sometimes he would not come out for an entire weekend. This fact alone did not raise any alarm bells for his family, Mark had stated the untruth that he was doing his holiday homework in preparation for the year to come. He had wanted to achieve a high ATAR score. This was the score that was used by universities for acceptance into courses. It was also an estimate of the percentage of the population that you outperformed. Mark had high expectations for himself, so it came as no surprise to anyone that he was getting off to a good start. But the truth of the matter was that he was neither studying nor getting off to a good start.

As the school year commenced his family and teachers had considered the changes in Mark's behaviours to be due to the normal pressures of the impending final year of school. Mark had, after all, always been a high achiever and there had never been any evidence to indicate that his behaviour was anything other than the fact he was focusing on his studies.

Hamish had not seen it. There had been *no* obvious signs alluding to the massive degree of emotional distress that Mark must have been experiencing, all alone, unobserved.

Hamish was now tortured by the nagging questions of "why?"

Why it was that Mark had chosen to keep his feelings to himself?

Why had he, his best friend, not been able to see it?

Why did Mark think this was an option, a solution to his problems?

Why?

His mind was screaming WHY?

The questions in his mind were unrelenting.

After the first month of school Hamish had become aware that his friend had been overly consumed by his constant need to check in to social media, chat rooms, Snap Chat, Instagram to name a few. His friend's disposition was becoming more and more agitated and negative. His phone was never far from his hand and he seemed to be becoming addicted to checking it. If he couldn't sign in or log in or if his phone went flat, he would become noticeably anxious, to the point that even Hamish was growing concerned for his friend.

Hamish was also in the chat groups to a lesser extent, and he could see the amount of time his friend was spending scrolling through, and becoming overly involved in negative opinions and posts, some of which were directly referring to him in the most negative of ways.

Hamish had spoken to Mark about it. They had talked about the fact that he was worried that it was becoming unhealthy, in fact he had raised his concerns on more than one occasion. The response from Mark was always the same and in the end this is what they had argued about.

At the time of his death, Mark was in the habit of being on his phone all hours of the day, even during class time, and all hours of the night.

The constant notifications which disturbed and interrupted his sleep, had over time cumulatively created sleep deprivation that was contributing to overwhelming feelings of anxiety, that worsened day by day. Social media and all it entailed had become a compulsion for Mark. Hamish had accused him of being overly involved. Mark's response was one of denial; he resolutely protested that he was fine. He just didn't want to "miss out" on what was being said. To do so would have been dangerous for a tall poppy like Mark Fredrick. How would he know who was saying what and to whom? He had to keep checking, but the more he did, the worse he felt.

"You've got FOMO, Mark Fredrick!" he heard them cry.

Hamish often wondered if Mark's mother had any idea of the extent to which Mark was being dragged in to the murkiness of the internet. He had even considered talking to his own mother about it, but for some reason he had not. Perhaps he didn't really want to believe his friend had a problem. Mark, who was always the most responsible of them all; if he of all people could not adequately manage the effects of social media and the stress of modern life, then surely there was no hope for anyone. Would Mark still be alive if he had spoken up? Hamish felt the knot in his stomach tighten again.

There was so much negativity in some of the posts that it seemed to represent a mass group consciousness whereby everyone apparently wanted to be the most outrageous as they sought to outdo each other in their negativity and criticism. Naturally those involved in these groups had to keep coming back to ensure they were not the butt of what was in fact cyber-bullying. The kind of insidious bullying that nobody was protected from. The kind of bullying that could follow you right into your bedroom and continue unnoticed until it was too late.

It had seemed to Hamish that there was no social responsibility for the things that were posted by these strangers masquerading as friends on these sites. Who was monitoring these dangerous conversations? Who was responsible for the inevitable hurt that was often felt by those who were targeted or those who could never live up to the edited version of reality, that was presented as normal, in a world that was anything *but* normal? A world where it seemed everyone was a success and everyone had all the answers. A world where everyone had the right to say whatever they wanted, no matter whom they hurt along the way. A world where nobody took responsibility for the damage caused. In this world, the words spoken by faceless individuals in a cyber distorted reality would never be the words spoken to anyone in person.

Who was responsible for all of that? How was an 18-year-old young man supposed to make sense of any of it, this 'virtual reality' that was so far removed from actual reality, when he was totally immersed in it and could not see a way out?

Mark was undoubtedly addicted and it was no different to drug addiction. He got the same buzz from his social media hit and the same sense of relief and satisfaction when he checked in. He got the same surge of serotonin through his body that kept him coming back for more by checking his posts, by seeing how many likes, by monitoring who had commented, it *was* like a drug.

Hamish could see his friend changing before his very eyes, but even Hamish could not see just how far his friend had sunk into the soullessness and negativity of the World Wide Web. He was progressively sinking into a depression based on digital information overload and overwhelm, and his addictive and relentless need to be a part of it all.

* * *

Mark had been finding it so difficult to keep up with all the responsibilities of life, that initially the online world seemed appealing. It had seemed like a fun escape from all of life's pressures; Somewhere that he could just be himself, just Mark–not the school captain, not the V.C.E. student, not the state athlete, not the star football player–just Mark.

This apparent reprieve from the real world was not to last long however. The social media demons and demands that he had begun to experience over time, continued to lead him directly into a state of unresolvable anxiety and depression, from which there was no retreat. It followed him everywhere: at school, at the track, at home and even into the sanctity of his own bedroom in the middle of the night. Sound sleep had become a thing of the past, and that had made way for broken and interrupted sleep patterns necessary to keep informed of important status updates. The increasing feeling of malaise compounded everything for Mark. Feelings of negativity inundated him, to the point he felt as if he was drowning under the weight of it all, but who could he tell? And what would he say? There was nothing concrete to see, there *was* nothing real to show for these cyber pressures—but they were real for Mark, and they were felt by him in a truly destructive and palpable way.

It had seemed to Mark that the worse his developing social media addiction made him feel, the more he experienced a compulsion to get back online. He needed to see what was being posted; he had to ensure it was not he who was being targeted that day. The time he was spending on his devices was beginning to affect everything: his schooling, his sport and his friendships. As time went by, the overwhelming repetitive thoughts and feelings kept leading him back to the same behaviours that were causing him to feel overwhelmed in the first place. Useless hours upon hours were wasted scrolling and ruminating, ruminating and scrolling, and for the first time in his life Mark Fredrick felt like he didn't measure up.

He was excluded from many conversations which only served to add to his growing anxiety and developing sense of paranoia. Were they discussing him? Why was he being excluded? Were they belittling him or disparaging him? He had seen some comments openly criticising him. Some were downright hateful. Mark was a tall poppy, and there were many that wanted to trivialise and underrate his achievements. It was almost as though you were allowed to achieve success, but not too much. Too much success was seen as showing off or being 'up yourself.' What did that mean, anyway? Mark had never felt 'up himself,' quite the opposite in fact; he had always believed his natural gifts were a product of good genetics. How could you be 'up-yourself' about something that really had nothing to do with you? He was simply the recipient of very good luck, nothing more, nothing less.

* * *

Hamish had been completely unaware that his friend had emotionally deteriorated to this lowest of points; naturally he would never have deserted him, but he *was* becoming concerned. His friend's whole manner had changed. He was becoming rude, impatient and short tempered. Hamish had not seen this side of his friend before, so when concerns were raised and Mark had told his best friend to "fuck off and leave him alone," Hamish, who was feeling less than tolerant with his friend's outbursts, thought he would teach him a lesson, and he did just that, he walked away.

Now, as he lay in bed hopelessly lamenting that fateful decision, Hamish felt the weight of the world weighing down upon him. Was this his fault? He could have made a difference, if only he hadn't walked away. The guilt was unbearable, and now he would never know.

* * *

Mark stood in his best friend's room. He could see Hamish lying in his bed facing the wall and he could actually feel his pain and remorse. Mark looked for Grace, and she was immediately there.

He now knew better than to ask if there was anything he could do to help his friend, and so he simply surrendered to what he was witnessing. As he acknowledged his friend's pain, he understood his ripple. He also found the insight in that moment to not only forgive his friend, but also to forgive himself. As Mark completely surrendered to that moment, he focused on the strong feelings he had for his dear friend who was right before him, and as he did, he found that he was suddenly enveloped by an all-encompassing emotion; it was the purest love that was nothing short of heavenly. It was as though his heart had opened up and the love he had previously felt was amplified and instantaneously seemed to pour out of his soul toward his friend.

As Hamish lay in his bed, he suddenly felt an extraordinarily comforting warmth that seemed to flow through him and all around him. It was as though his body had been submerged in the most relaxing warm bath which had caused every bit of muscular tension to immediately melt away. For the first time in an entire week he felt relaxed and he couldn't explain why. Perhaps exhaustion had finally hit him, but it did not feel like exhaustion. He turned his head and looked directly towards Mark, but saw nothing. He couldn't quite define what the feeling was that had made him turn around, but it was almost as though he expected someone to be there. Nobody was there, but he had definitely sensed a welcoming warmth within the room that was enormously comforting to him. His thoughts went to Mark, and for the first time since Mark's death, Hamish smiled. There was a definite sense of Mark in the room. Hamish quietly whispered his name.

"Mark?"

Of course there was no answer, and Hamish did not expect there to be. The thought that perhaps his friend may have been paying him a visit from beyond this world was something he would never admit to anyone, but this secret thought was comforting and allowed him to believe that perhaps his friend was going to be all right now no matter where he was.

8

MR. GREGORY PRESTON

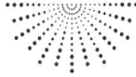

I t was at 8:45 am, Wednesday 27th March on the morning after the funeral of Mark Fredrick when Principal Greg Preston once again was seated in his office at the Green Valley Secondary School. He was preparing for his day and wondering how he could help his students and his staff begin the painful process of resuming life at school without their captain, Mark Fredrick. All he knew was that he had to do something to make a difference. Something that would help students like Mark to recognise the early warning signs of dangerous mental health issues and seek help before it was too late.

The phone on his desk rang three times. He answered with his usual professionalism. There was a slight tinge of sadness in his usually unharried voice; on any other day it may have been mistaken for weariness.

"Gregory Preston speaking," were the only words the principal uttered before he heard the distinct click of the call being disconnected. The message had been short and succinct.

"There are no further details at this stage," the disembodied voice on the other end of the phone had said before hanging up.

Exhaustion flooded through Principal Preston's body as he sat at his desk staring blankly at the wall ahead of him, trying desperately to comprehend the gravity of the information he had just received. He had just been informed of another teenage death by suicide. This time it was a thirteen-year-old girl from the junior school who had been found dead by her own hand. This was unconscionable.

The principal of Green Valley High sat at his desk, stunned once again by the delivery of *more* tragic news.

This young girl, Stacey Wilson, had been experiencing schoolyard bulling for some time. It had been dealt with at the school level, but unfortunately the degree of a problem such as this, is often sadly hidden from sight. It can follow students home into the sanctuary and safety of their own bedrooms and continue on unobserved, often until it is too late.

Stacey had been part of a cross-the-ages school initiative, whereby Year Twelve students were given an opportunity to spend a day in the life of a Year Seven student. It was an initiative and an invitation to support and buddy up with them for the entire semester, helping to ensure a smoother transition into the secondary years. For many in the past, this opportunity had provided the chance for the Year Seven students to learn and be inspired by the Year Twelve students; surprisingly, the Year Twelve students were benefiting just as much. They enjoyed the additional personal benefits of being a mentor and a resource person.

Stacey, partly due to the fact she had been having difficulty settling in to secondary school, and partly because she had been struggling to deal with a divisive group of girls and the associated bullying issues, was partnered up with someone who was seen to be the most appropriate. Someone who could support and lead her by example. Someone who was a natural born leader and mentor. Stacey Wilson had been partnered with Green Valley's school captain, Mark Fredrick.

Greg Preston hung up the phone and was unable to move.

Oh my GOD, what have I done? he thought.

For the second time in two weeks he had been given the news that one of his students had taken their own life.

Shit, SHIT, SHIT, SHIT, SHIT!

He was screaming internally, but no sound escaped him. Why had he not thought of Stacey throughout all this trauma, why had he not considered how she had taken the tragic news that *her* buddy had killed himself?

You stupid bloody idiot! *He scolded himself inwardly.*

It appeared to him as though his world had suddenly stopped–or perhaps it was *he,* who was frozen solid, unable to move, unable to process reality. In that moment it seemed as though he was unable to process anything at all. He was well aware that the world was busily going on around him and he wondered why. How was it even possible that anything was continuing on as normal at this moment of complete devastation. As *his* world stood still, he wondered what he was meant to do with this painful information. The Green Valley School community was already reeling from the death of a boy they all knew and loved, but how could anyone process or make sense of the deaths of *two* children, *by their own hands*?

Not an accident, not a mistake. How?

Children, they were only bloody children. They had their whole lives ahead of them. He felt dizzy, sick, somehow detached from his surroundings, almost as though he were in a tunnel, being pulled far away from the reality of the world around him. Somewhere in the distance he could clearly hear the sounds of children at play, which puzzled him. Again he wondered just how it was that life *could* be going on as normal? He felt confused, somehow numb. Nothing made sense.

How was it that we were all taking this in our stride?

What is happening to the world when a thirteen-year-old child believes the only viable option is to kill herself?

What were they thinking?

What terrible things were they experiencing in this world where they should have been able to just be children?

What would make them take such an action?

What kind of a world have we created for these children when this is now a normal, somehow accepted, part of life?

These thoughts and more bombarded him, striking him like a punch to the stomach that winded him. Thoughts hit him with such ferocity that he was shocked and stunned by their impact. He was under attack by the relentless questions now being fired at him with the speed and accuracy of a machine gun, questions for which sadly he had no answers.

He had no idea how this had happened, but he did know one thing; he knew that he had unwittingly played a part. He, of all people, had *certainly* contributed to this epic tragedy. He was a leader in the community, a teacher of children, and this was a privilege and a responsibility that he *never* took for granted; but nonetheless, now under his watch, children were killing themselves. Just when he thought he could not be any more devastated, this latest news shocked him to his very core.

The phone dropped out of his hand, almost involuntarily. He did not think to pick it up. Greg Preston lowered his head to his hands, feeling utterly gutted and incredulous, as he held the heavy weight of his head, he began to cry.

* * *

Mark Fredrick stood in silence in the office of his principal, unobserved, as now *he* observed all. He glanced about looking for Grace, who was naturally instantly by his side. He felt her loving presence penetrate through his energy field and embrace him as he looked on at the scene unfolding in front of him. He had never before seen this strong and resilient man, his school principal, Mr. Gregory Preston, cry.

He wanted to let him know that he was all right.

He wanted to tell him of the love that existed here.

He wanted to let him know that he was not dead.

Most of all, he wanted him to know he was sorry.

He wanted to relieve this man, whose only mission in life was to teach and to lead, of the burden of guilt he suffered over the deaths of two students; whose deaths were never his fault.

He also wondered if he in some way was responsible for the death of another young student who had looked up to him as a leader and a role model. As these thoughts permeated his consciousness, he glanced towards Grace.

"Everyone is on their own journey, Mark," she expressed.

"Everyone has things to experience and learn on this earthly plane, and most importantly, everyone has free will to do what he chooses, just as you had free will, Mark."

* * *

9am on Thursday 28th of March. Two days after Mark Fredrick's funeral and one day after the tragic news that yet another student from his school had taken her own life. Mr. Gregory Preston, school principal of Green Valley Secondary College sat in his office contemplating what he was about to do. His instinct told him he needed to act fast; he had to do something tangible, something that would really make a difference. More than that, he needed to be true to himself, he had to find a solution to this insidious and ever-growing problem. An issue that seemed to be like an untameable serpent, suddenly erupting from the dark depths of the unknown and the unseen, to wreak havoc on all that witnessed it. Once the beast had made its appearance, it could never be unseen, never be forgotten. This beast's devastation had been felt by the entire community of Green Valley. Greg Preston had to implement strategies that would create a safety net to catch any student teetering on the mental health tightrope, hovering just above the beast that would surely devour them should they fall into the dark abyss, unsupported and unprotected.

He had called an extraordinary assembly at which he was about to address all school staff, including the school's teaching faculty and the entire student body. There would be no excuses, everyone was to be present. An email was sent out to all school parents and guardians inviting them to attend. Due to the numbers that had responded and presented themselves on this Thursday morning, the crowd in the auditorium had overflowed into the courtyard, where Greg Preston's address would be heard over the school's loud speaker system.

The school had been closed by necessity two days earlier as nearly all here present at this unscheduled assembly had represented Green Valley Secondary College at Mark Fredrick's funeral. The principal had made some decisions about how the school, as a whole, needed to move forward from these terrible events. He was aware that everyone here had been affected by these grave events in some way. Everyone present that day knew that there was about to be an announcement of importance, but none knew exactly what it was to be.

Mr. Preston appeared on the stage area in the main college auditorium, and as he did, the entire audience of parents, students, teachers, assistants and secretaries fell silent. There was none of the usual light-hearted whispers, followed by teachers 'shushing.' In its place, an immediate and respectful silence filled the air, as everyone present waited to hear what their principal was about to say.

Their principal stood in silence. It was apparent he was trying to compose himself. To those looking on it seemed as if he was about to cry, something that had *never* shown itself in this previously emotionally strong man who always seemed to cope effortlessly with anything that occurred at the school. He had an air of professionalism and confidence about him that always left the recipient of his attentions feeling that Greg Preston could cope with just about anything.

As he stood before the entire school, Greg felt an unfamiliar feeling of nervousness combined with the deepest regret. He now had an unshakeable vision of what must happen from this day forward in his school, and it was imperative that he delivered his message succinctly. He had been feeling overcome with the burden of knowing that he may, in some way, have unknowingly contributed to the weight of extraneous expectations that had led his school captain to do the unthinkable. This was a mistake he would never make again.

He cleared his throat and began to speak. He said that he wished firstly to express how proud he was of each and every one of them, in terms of how they had coped with the unprecedented events of the past two weeks, and how they all had presented themselves as they represented their school at such an emotionally difficult time; the funeral of their school captain. He said that he wanted to acknowledge the trauma and upset that each of them had been experiencing over the last week. *Trauma, he knew, that was now to be compounded by the unfathomable tragedy of yet another loss of precious young life yesterday.* He again cleared his throat and took a deep breath.

"I once again have the most tragic news to convey to you on this very sad day. News that many of you will already know, but information that will come as a shock to many others. Yesterday I received a terrible phone call that revealed to me that yet another Green Valley Secondary College student has done the unthinkable. Yesterday,

Stacey Wilson from Year Seven was found dead. It is with great sadness I announce that Stacy took her own life."

With tears welling in his eyes he expressed the deepest sadness that he had not been aware of the obvious pressures and unhappiness that had led to this terrible outcome.

"For those of you who did not know of this tragedy, I apologise if this news is distressing to you, but I do not apologise for stating it as a truth here, loud and clear. For too long we, as a school, and we as a community have shied away from having these discussions. We have talked about it in hushed tones behind closed doors as though it was some kind of a shame, on family, on school and on community. I stand here today to say it is only a shame on family, on school and on community when we *do not* speak of these matters. I am ashamed that I have not spoken more clearly after Mark's death, but I will never make that mistake again. Stacey Wilson may be here today if I had, and that is a travesty that I will never forgive myself for. As for Mark Fredrick, I do not blame myself, but I accept my part in unknowingly adding to Mark's emotional burden as school captain, something that I should have been more aware of. These have been the most terrible events that have happened at our school during my time as principal, and I want to make a promise to all present that I will do my utmost to ensure this never happens again."

He carried on to say that there were pressures that were seen and unseen that had been a part in both these deaths.

"There is not a person here that will be unaffected by these events, and I would like to invite you all to continue to take advantage of the school counsellors that have been provided by not only our own school, but also by the surrounding schools and the education department."

"In front of all here present, I want to make a declaration that *this must never happen again*. As we move forward from these tragedies as a school united, I intend for us all to work together to ensure that anyone struggling with emotional burdens, that seem too heavy to carry on their own, can feel free to come forward and ask for help."

"All of you are growing up in a world that is unlike the world that most adults in this room grew up in. There are additional pressures from social media and associated bullying that can occur anywhere and follow you home into the privacy of your own bedroom. Today I make a promise to all present that bullying in any form will never be tolerated at Green Valley Secondary College. This is now and forever after a safe zone, and I invite any person who is struggling with overwhelming emotional issues to knock on *my* door. Confidentiality will always be assured. I also invite any bystander to report any bullying or to alert a teacher about anyone that they think is in need of help. I want to say clearly that it is never ok to be a silent bystander. Silence *can* and *does* cost lives. I want to cultivate a culture of compassion and consideration in our school, and know this: it is always better to risk losing a friend and saving their life by telling a teacher, than it is to lose both by remaining silent. I will always make myself available and I will always assist in getting any person the help they need, to deal with whatever they may be going through."

"I have stood in the guard of honour of one of our beloved students this week, and my heart bleeds that I will once again be required to do this next week. I want to say categorically that, after next week, I never again want to have to stand in the guard of honour of any student who has taken their own life because he or she thought there was no other option. I never want any student at this school or any other school to feel that there is no alternative, because together we *can* find solutions."

Together we can make a difference.

Together we can be there for each other.

Together we can get through all things.

Together we are strong.

"Today, we need to stand united and send a clear message to all, that it is *not* a disgrace to admit you are struggling, it is *not* a disgrace to ask for help, in fact it is probably the bravest thing you will ever do."

With tears beginning to well in his eyes he said with the most heart-felt sincerity he could summon, "Today I stand before you as an example to all, completely transparent and honest, to express to you that I am struggling with this." He then fell silent for at least a minute as he tried to compose himself enough to speak again. He cleared his throat and continued, "It is important to let you know that I have questioned *my own* actions in all of this, as I'm sure many of you will also do. I have had to ask myself the hard questions Why did I not see this coming? Why was I not alerted to the fact that there was some-thing so desperately wrong with a young man so closely under my direct care? What did I do or not do, that may have contributed to the death of now two students, Stacey Wilson and Mark Fredrick?"

"I want you all to understand that it is a privilege for me, as your prin-cipal, to have you all attend our school, Green Valley Secondary College, and for the trust that your parents or guardians put in us to care for you, and support not only your educational requirements, but also your social and emotional needs.

I have wondered how it was that I did not recognise that Mark Fredrick was so troubled, and this is something that I myself will need to look further in to. The reason I am telling you this is because there are always repercussions from a terrible event like this. I say this to you all, so that you get the message clearly; it is okay not to be okay *all* the time. It is okay to feel sad, it is okay to have difficulty making sense of life and it is okay to have difficulty making sense of this terrible tragedy, no matter who you are.

Most importantly it is okay to ask for help.

Please, if there is *one* thing that we all learn from this let it be that *it is ok to ask for help.*"

"I have thought long and hard about how we can now safely and respectfully move forward, united in our grief, with the knowledge that we have all gained from these terrible tragedies. I understand that the school is reeling from the events of the last two weeks, as is our local community; the full impacts will probably not be known for some time, but as your principal, I really want to minimise the impact within the school. I want us to never forget. We must learn from this so that it does not happen again."

"I have decided that as a sign of respect to Mark, for the rest of this year, I will not appoint another school captain. The existing vice captains and the teaching faculty, including myself, will attend to any school captain duties that arise. Next year there will be two school captains elected, one male and one female, and two vice captains, one male and one female. Never again will one student have to attend to all the duties involved with captainship on their own. All captains will personally meet with me once a term to ensure that they are coping with their studies and their extracurricular activities. I have also gained approval from the board of directors to place an advertisement this week seeking a permanent school counsellor. I will also be advertising a new position for a school chaplain. Both position descriptions will be to provide care for all students and staff. I whole-heartedly encourage all of you to utilise these services when and if required. I want you all to know that there is confidential help available and nobody ever needs to struggle on alone."

"Our school will lead the way for anti-bullying and I would ask that you all consider, as a student group, what else we can do to ensure that this never happens again in our school. Suicide—that word everyone shies away from saying—is what we need to talk about, and I *will* stand up here and say it out loud. *Suicide took our school captain* and we need to all be part of a conversation that is loud and clear. One teenage death by suicide is one too many."

"I am now asking anyone here who would like to participate in a confidential discussion forum with the purpose of creating strategies that can be implemented within our school, to consider attending weekly meetings that will commence in the week after Stacey Green's funeral. Our agenda will be to create strategies that will flag potentially concerning behaviours before they become overwhelming; workable ideas that can be implemented into our school to ensure that no other student feels that suicide is the only option. This forum will create much needed conversations about respect and compassion that will allow anybody who is struggling to know and understand that they are not alone. Ideas that may save the lives of your fellow students. I want to hear from *you,* my students. I want, and need, to understand the issues and the pressures, so together we can work toward solutions. Teachers wishing to participate are naturally welcome, but this needs to be directed by the students, *for* the students."

Gregory Preston took a deep breath as he looked about the auditorium. He had their attention.

"I believe nobody understands the pressures, the triggers and the emotional burdens of today's students and adolescents better than you, the students. There is definitely a place for adults to make rules and decisions for children and adolescents, but I do not feel this is one of them. I truly trust and believe that you will rise to this challenge and create something that perhaps can be implemented in all schools to benefit all students. Naturally there will be agreement from all members present to maintain the confidentiality of any personal information discussed in the group, so that no topic is off limits. Topics including the more destructive practices and issues experienced on social media, to social drug usage and its effects will be discussed. There will be no judgment in this group. Any person brave enough to speak on these issues will be assured confidentiality, which will be respected in every circumstance except those of potential danger to any student."

"Please take some time to think about it. I want to invite open discussion to plan for the way forward. This will be a student-led initiative. You, the students of Green Valley Secondary College, have the answers to the problems only *you* really understand. Together we can uncover the solutions and implement them into our school—and in doing so lives will be changed, lives will be saved."

"Vale Mark Fredrick."

"Vale Stacey Wilson."

"Your deaths will not be in vain."

"Thank you," he concluded.

Everyone in the auditorium stood in respectful silence, then a single clap sounded followed by another until the whole of the student body joined and applauded their principal as he turned and left the stage.

9

THE STUDENTS UNITE

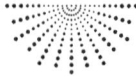

I t was 1 pm exactly, lunchtime on Tuesday 9th April. Over a week had passed, and sadly yet another student funeral had been attended by the principal of Green Valley Secondary College, since he had addressed the school at the unscheduled assembly where he publicly declared his intention to take action on the serious issue of teen suicide.

Gregory Preston was a gentle yet strong man, but the events of the last few weeks had truly rocked him to his core, such that he had taken time to reflect seriously upon his own actions; the things he did and did not do that may in any way have contributed to the deaths of two of his students. He reflected on his ability to move on from this, if indeed this was even possible for him in his current position. He had no doubt that he would never be able to continue in his role if this were ever to happen again. It would be a blow to the education department of huge proportions to lose such a man, but it was his firm belief that he was not doing his job if he could not protect the most vulnerable children under his care.

He sat in the auditorium, not knowing what would happen from here. He didn't know who, if anyone, would turn up to address this festering issue within his school. He hoped students would come, but he would have to wait and see.

Teachers were welcome, but this was to be student-run so the adults could get some understanding and insight as to what the current problems and issues were that were pushing children to the brink and beyond. Whatever those reasons were, it had to stop now.

He waited. Minutes felt like hours as the ticking of the clock high on the auditorium wall was the only sound to break the silence. The clock hands moved minute by minute to five past one; nobody had arrived, but then the sound of a single set of footsteps was audible on the highly polished wooden floor of the anteroom, just outside the auditorium. He looked up in expectation and was somewhat deflated to see it was only Mrs Foster, the Year Twelve coordinator. Naturally he was pleased to see her in the emptiness of the hall, but he was hoping for a significant student presence here today. Surely they were also concerned. Surely they did not think that this situation was acceptable, or was this in fact the point? Did they accept the situation as something they could do nothing about, just a part of daily life as they knew it?

He had held such hopes for this group. He had hoped it would be the catalyst for immense change in the social culture of his school, but not just within this school–he hoped it would create a model that could be replicated for all schools. For the sake of the children this must be done right. His eyes met those of Mrs. Foster and he smiled but his disappointment was obvious.

"They will come," she said. "They are probably just getting their lunch."

At eight minutes past one came the sound of voices and many sets of footsteps. Greg Preston again looked up, this time with relief; this was the undeniable sound of students entering, en masse. Principal Preston smiled to himself. He should have known that they would come in a group, safety in numbers when coming to meet with the principal was always the best idea for 14 to 18-year-old students.

"Right, you are here. Thank you all for coming."

"You all know why we are here, and I would like to desist with the formalities and get down to it."

"I think these meetings should go for approximately 30 minutes, so you still have some time to do the other things you need to do during lunch time. However, I will be guided by you all. This is your forum."

"There are some ground rules but the main one is that of confidentiality. Unless someone is in danger of injuring himself or someone else, your confidentiality must be assured. To ensure this confidentiality on behalf of other students, I would ask that we speak in general terms and avoid using specific student names. I would also ask that anything personal raised by any student in confidence here, be respected and not repeated outside of this group. I want everyone to feel safe to discuss anything they think is a problem, or anything they think may help. Do we all agree?"

There was unanimous consent from all present.

"Thank you."

"I believe this is essential to the open communication I hope will be achieved within this group. As your school principal, some of the things discussed in this group may be ethically challenging for me as I also have a responsibility to your parents, therefore, I would ask that all personal discussions be in third person and direct reference to individuals be avoided. I trust that each and every one of you would report through the correct channels any concerns that may be dangerous or life threatening. This is not the forum for that. Here we are trail blazers. We are solution seekers. We are explorers of the facts, and as I said at the assembly, I truly believe that together we can make a difference. *You* can make a difference. Does everyone here understand the ground rules, and what it is we are hoping to achieve?"

Again, there was a resounding yes.

"Great—let's get started. Who wants to begin?"

Silence.

"Kristen, how about you? Can you get this ball rolling? What concerns you most as a 17-year-old girl living in the world today?"

"Well, can I talk about social media? I think it is so bad for people's mental health. I really think this is a major issue. I know Mark was getting more and more heavily involved in it. Oh sorry—I said Mark. Can I say Mark? I know you said don't use names?"

"Yes, I think that it is fine to say Mark. We need to honour him through this process, but please, when names are used, we need to be very respectful."

Kristen began to cry.

"I'm sorry," she said. "I'm really struggling with all of this. This is why I thought it was so important to come today. So many of us in Year Twelve just can't come to terms with this. We have no idea how this could have happened; we just don't know why. I often think if only I had known, perhaps I could have made a difference. Maybe he would still be alive. If only I had asked him how he was. If only I had known. I can't believe it. It's such a waste, an incredible waste. Mark of all people had so much to live for. He was so talented, so alive and so involved with life—and now he's dead and it is totally insane." She took a moment to blow her nose, before she continued.

"The reality is that I didn't know and I probably wouldn't have known what to do even if I did. God, what if I did know and did nothing because nobody ever believes that this is going to ever happen, and perhaps that's part of the problem. I need to know what the warning signs are. I want to know what I need to look out for, and what I need to do. This is what I hope to see come out of this group. We all need to know about the warning signs and what we should do. Every student in this school needs to know because so many of us feel in some way responsible. We feel we let Mark down when he needed us most, and now we all have to live with that. Like, forever! Personally, I really need to talk about this in a constructive way, not the school yard gossip way. I need to know what went wrong."

"That's all," she added sheepishly.

"Kristen, thank you for getting us started. I know many of you feel the same, and I hope that this group will be a forum for discussion on all of these important issues. I completely agree with you, we need to get conversations started and we have to educate everyone through these discussions, from the students in Year Seven right through to Year Twelve. We also the need to educate teachers and all school ancillary staff on these matters. We all need to learn and we all need to educate others—and it starts today. Thank you, Kristen."

"Would anyone else like to speak?"

"I would like to," said a young girl. "My name is Jacqueline. I am..," she paused, "I *was* a good friend of Stacey Wilson."

It was clear this young Year Seven girl was valiantly fighting to hold back tears.

"Stacey was being bullied on social media. She was being targeted by students who were too gutless to speak to her face and I'm angry."

"Thank you, Jacqueline, for sharing. I'm so sorry for your loss. I know there are many serious issues that we and every other school are facing. What I would like to have happen here is to illuminate these issues. To bring them out of the darkness and highlight them so that you, the students, with what you know that I do not, can brainstorm as to what the solutions may be and we can figure out how we can implement them. It is one thing to know there is a problem, but it's quite another to plan for change, and then to take action to make those changes. We will do this, and, when we do, I would like us to meet to evaluate how the changes are going and if we need to make more changes."

"I would like you all to think about how we can begin to fix this. How can we ensure no other students feel the way your friends felt? Let's direct our conversations towards the issues. Jacqueline, this will definitely be on our agenda for discussion and I value your input, thank you for your honesty. I also would like to suggest that it may be good for you to see one of the school counsellors to talk about how you are feeling, would that be ok with you?"

"Yes," she said as the tear that had taken her every effort to hold back finally escaped and ran down her cheek.

"Ok," said Mr. Preston. "Let's talk about social media then."

Rebecca, another Year Twelve student began.

"The real issue with social media is that it is *not* real. Nothing is real, yet we all hold ourselves up to have to compete with this virtual edited world. We all know it's just edited reality, yet we all do it. The pictures people upload are all edited, everybody knows it— but we still do it, it's so hard to explain. There's a compulsion to outdo each other. People at school post pictures that have been deliberately selected, photoshopped or face tuned so that we are constantly comparing ourselves to an edited version of the world. A part of us knows this isn't real, but there is another part of us that is left feeling less than, or not good enough. How can we ever compare ourselves to edited perfection? It's one thing to know your friend has photoshopped her photos, but famous people we don't know do it too, and the question is, what is real and what is not? Everyone only posts the good pics or the edited bits, and, of course, anyone's life is going to look amazing if you only get to see the good bits. Everything else is edited out and thus, it does not exist. If it doesn't get posted, it never happened. We see supermodels posting their perfect bodies, when it's their job to work on their body for hours each day and still, even these photos are edited, how can anyone live up to that? How can anyone be happy when this is in our face 24/7? It is a gold standard that is completely ridiculous and unattainable for most, yet we are led to believe that this is the only way to feel happy. This is what it takes, and it's not possible. It's not attainable."

"Are they really happy, do you think?" asked Principal Preston.

"Probably not, but if *they* can't be happy with all that, what hope do we have? Body image *is* a major issue."

"It used to just be magazines and billboards, but now anyone can do anything with their photos. People have apps on their phones that can blur their face, or whiten their teeth. They can make their eyes wider, their waist thinner. It's really crazy. You can move your eyebrow inwards, upwards; you can change their shape—you can do anything. People become obsessed with their cyber appearance."

'What is the impact of all this on you?"

"It causes anxiety, so much anxiety. If you don't upload what you are doing, how will people know it's happened?"

"Which people?"

"People who follow us."

"So, strangers that follow you?"

"No, well, yes, some we haven't met, but they *are* friends, you know what I mean? Social media friends. They comment on our posts and you like and comment on theirs."

"How many 'friends' are we talking about?"

"It depends on the group or page you are on; there's a lot. Some have hundreds, some have thousands."

"So, there are thousands of 'friends' that you are checking in on, that you need to follow, and you also need to upload stories and pictures to your own pages to keep all these friends, is that right?" Gregory Preston clarified, scratching his head.

"Yes. Something like that." Her face flushed.

"It sounds like all this would take a great deal of time"

"It really does, and there is a pressure feeling I get if I haven't posted or checked in for a few hours. A feeling like I'll get left behind, or miss out on something important. It's also really important to post what you are doing. You know, if I go into the city or to a function, I need to post it, because people won't know I'm there if I don't."

"And what will happen if they don't know you are there?"

"Sure. You know I can say who cares, but there's a part of me that does care; a part that knows what others think, 'no pics, and it didn't happen.' It's as if the pics are the proof, or else nobody believes you. Naturally they are all edited. There is this constant pressure to upload so it gives the impression that I'm living this great life. For example, I may only go to Crown Casino once a year, but every time I do I'll upload it, so there's this illusion that my life is exciting. I am aware that so much of this sounds ridiculous, but this is the reality of the world we live in, and this is just one aspect of it. So many kids are affected in different ways." She paused and looked around the auditorium before continuing. Many of the other students were nodding in agreement.

"Mark wasn't interested in changing his appearance or editing his photos," she continued, "But he was getting overly involved in social media in other ways. Even as I say the words, 'social media,' I am acutely aware that it is in fact anti-social media. It causes separation and it is the perfect forum for anti-social behaviour, as Jacqueline already said. The problem is that, although we all know this, it somehow drags you in. To be honest, I actually think it affects our ability to concentrate, because of the constant pings and interruptions. I feel like my ability to focus on my study has also been affected. There is always this feeling that I should just check in for a few minutes, but minutes turn into hours as I scroll from one thing to another. I know it's not healthy, but the more I do it, the more I seem to *need* to do it. I kid myself that I'm choosing these behaviours, but I'm afraid to admit, sometimes it feels like I just have to get online. It sometimes feels like an addiction that I really can't control."

"Thank you for your honesty, Rebecca. I'm beginning to get a clearer picture of some of the areas of concern. You have raised many issues that we definitely need to discuss."

"Anyone else?"

"Drugs are a real issue," said Catherine, a Year Twelve girl who had, until now, remained silent in the corner.

"Not that either of these two deaths that we are discussing had anything to do with drugs, but in general it is a serious contributing factor, and I think we should discuss it."

"Thank you, Catherine. Please continue," said Mr. Preston.

"So many kids from every year level are taking drugs. I'm really sad to say it, and perhaps it may come as a surprise to you, Mr. Preston, but there is an epidemic in this school and in every other school in the state, perhaps the country. Anyone who thinks there is not is kidding themselves. You consider this to be a good school. Well, I can tell you that at least fifty percent of the Year 12 students have taken drugs at least once; many take them regularly. It is widely accepted, almost expected, that drugs will be readily available at most senior school parties. This is hugely affecting the mental health and well-being of so many students."

"I can categorically say that I personally have not taken drugs, possibly because my Mum is a psychologist who has worked in drug rehabilitation for fifteen years, but I *can* assure you, I have been offered many opportunities to partake. In my home, we have always talked openly and honestly about this topic. I am very aware of the real dangers because I have visited drug rehab clinics with my mum, and I have seen for myself the damage these drugs can cause. It is a real factor across the state that is implicated in teen depression and suicide. I think it needs to be raised in our discussions."

Greg Preston looked somewhat surprised at what he had just heard, but this is what he was here for, so he put aside his first instinct to disagree and invited Catherine to continue.

"I am aware that I'm putting myself out there by talking like this, but I can't be silent any more. It is hard for me to see so many students engaging in these risk-taking activities. Smart kids, who really think this rubbish is safe to take. I have even heard people say you can't overdose on MDMA...MDMA for God's sake, someone died last Saturday night from just one dose. My Dad is an accident and emergency nurse manager in one of the major city hospitals, and he and his colleagues have to deal with the reality of drug use every single day, and the impacts of that on the family and friends of the users."

"I hate it when I see my friends at parties getting completely wasted on substances that they have no idea about. They have no clue what is in these concoctions, no idea of the real dangers, or that they are playing Russian Roulette with their own lives every time they take stupid 'Molly' or 'Special K.' That's ketamine for those of you who don't know. Ketamine is an anaesthetic drug, a tranquilliser that can cause hallucinations and loss of consciousness and death. I know for a fact that many of the Year Twelve boys commonly take both these drugs combined with alcohol at parties; it scares me. The concoctions just seem to get worse and worse, and are often voluntarily ingested by idiotic boys who are looking for a bigger and bigger hit. I even heard the other day that the latest thing is called a "Kelvin Cline." This is when ketamine is mixed with cocaine! These ridiculous risks are being taken every weekend."

"In our school, this *is* a tragedy just waiting to happen," she continued on, "but there is a bigger picture here, that is directly related to our topic of suicide. This rubbish changes the pleasure receptors and the neurotransmitters in kids' brains permanently, so that it's nearly impossible for them to get a normal level of enjoyment out of every day activities anymore. These drugs are creating a generation of depressed kids who can't find any joy in life. Life becomes a sad, dark place for them, so they take even more drugs to feel any normal level of enjoyment."

"Ok, if what you are saying is true, then we have a bigger problem than I thought. This is very concerning, thank you for your honesty, Catherine."

"Our time is nearly up today, and I would like to commend you all for your bravery in speaking out. We will persevere—and we *will* find solutions. Let's meet here again at the same time next week and please, in the meantime, think of what we can do about these issues that might make a difference in creating change."

Gregory Preston was pleased to see his students hug and embrace each other at the end of the meeting. A great feeling of camaraderie seemed to have been born in the room that day.

* * *

Mark watched on from afar. He wanted them all to know what he was now beginning to know. He could see how so many of his fellow students were suffering. He wanted for them to be able to see through the earthly veil that blocked so many important realisations. He wanted them to know that earthly life is but a blink in the universal time realm, where time as they know it doesn't even exist. Here, where he was—and he still was not that sure where 'here' was—there are no heavy earthly emotions, like despair, grief, or blame. He wanted all of them to know that the only real emotions that remain are love, joy, peace and a sense of absolute harmony in all things. He now knew that there is no separation from *The Source*; we are all pure love and love is the answer to every question, every situation, to everything. *Oh my God, what a difference it would have made to him on Earth, if he had only known this then! Why didn't we all know this?*

He looked at Grace, her beautiful benevolent smile grew larger, but the joy did not come from her face—it radiated throughout her entire being as a heavenly glow that enriched his own understandings moment by moment as these realisations dawned upon him. He knew that there was a reason for everything. He understood for the first time that we were all here upon this Earth, on our own journeys, and that we were all here to enrich our souls and the soul of humanity. He now knew that it was our freedom of choice that enabled us to learn wisdom and contribute to the universal experience of this thing we called *life*.

When would the world see that what the universal experience really required right now was more love? Not hate, not grievance, not competitive comparison that only served to create even more separation. We are one: therefore there *is* no separation. We are whole, and we are love in its purest essence. Every problem can be healed with acceptance and love.

He wanted these students and teachers to know what *he* had never been aware of until these precious present moments; that we are supported and nurtured from the moment of our birth by a powerful universal source that knows all, sees all, and is capable of all. That source is a pure loving energy. Some call it God, some call it Buddha, some call it the Universe, but it is one and the same because there *is* only one. We are one, we are love, we are all: and that is enough. Every person *is* enough. If Mark had only known this, what a comfort it would have been and how it could have shone light upon his darkest moments.

* * *

Over the next few meetings plans were made and strategies designed to begin the process of change within the school. One of the wonderful changes initiated by the students was a complete ban on the use of social media during school hours. This initiative resulted in students having six-and-a-half hours a day that they could be free of the cyber world. All phones were to be left in lockers and were not to be used at school whether in class or at recess. An email was sent out to every parent and guardian about this new initiative with a view to promoting increased mental health outcomes for the students. The students were also asked to observe a turn off time of 9 pm. This was something the school could not control; however, parents were informed and encouraged to actively participate with their children in order to see this initiative succeed.

It was a great start. The students received a survey four weeks into the changes and the results were resoundingly positive. Students reported feeling less stressed and more able to relax at break times. Some reported better personal interactions, and others began to get more involved in social club activities and group sporting practices.

It was wonderful to observe. Greg Preston walked the school grounds and he could feel hope rising as he saw the changes were indeed making a significant difference. Where previously students would have been seated together in silent groups, eyes down, glued to their devices, now they were participating in conversations, in sporting activities, in life. There was a healthy integration of all year levels participating in group activities. There were basketballs and footballs being thrown and kicked. Some students were even running around playing games of tag, or initiating an impromptu athletic session down on the oval. The yard was alive with the energy of youth and it was such a pleasure to observe. Teachers had reported more enthusiasm in the classroom and less apathy. Parents were reporting students were getting more sleep and were brighter in the mornings. Greg Preston had to admit it, this had been a great success.

The drug issues were not so easy to address, but the group had made a good start by getting the school to talk even more about the dangers of drugs and what happens to the brain after drug use. A program of guest speakers was drawn up and experts in their specific fields were invited to speak at a whole-school assembly every term. Police, nurses, doctors, psychologists, ambulance paramedics and parents of teens who had died tragically, were all invited to speak.

The Year Nine program was changed to include a field trip to a major rehabilitation centre, where some of the residents would speak to students about the real story of drug and alcohol use. While half of them attended a day in this setting, the other half would spend their day in the emergency services sector, getting an understanding of the damage caused on the front line—not only to those taking drugs, but to those trying to save their lives.

The many changes Principal Preston and the students had created would gradually be assessed over time. He would never know the full implications of these changes, but if even one life could be saved by these actions, Greg Preston knew it would be worth it.

10

CHRISTINE: THE DECLINE

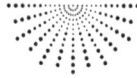

The weeks that followed Mark's funeral were marred by a heaviness that seemed to descend into the entire fabric of the Fredrick household. It even seemed to permeate through the walls creating a feeling of hopelessness such that even the house felt somehow heavy and sad. It was hard to describe this feeling; it was almost as if a tight band of depression surrounded the building itself, and anyone who entered would immediately be consumed by the grief of it all. Life as normal had ceased to exist within these walls.

In those early weeks after the funeral, the ladies from the local Christian school's auxiliary, having heard of Mark's fate, had presented at the front door offering to help the family in any way they could. They brought a casserole and a cake, and offered to pray for the family. Christine politely thanked them but then she took the gifts and abruptly, rather rudely, shut the door as one of the ladies attempted to say something further. She had no desire to chat politely to anyone anymore.

About the same time, one kind woman bearing an apple tea cake had asked Alex, who happened to answer the door on that occasion, if the family would mind if her sister's church group in Spain could also pray for them. Alex was really having a difficult time having faith in anything at the moment; life as he once knew it was now unrecognisable, and, in his quieter moments, he was definitely questioning how God could have allowed this to happen, but as he looked at the woman standing in front of him, he kept his opinions on such matters to himself. He actually just wanted her to leave, so he said, "Of course," accepting the cake graciously, then excusing himself and shutting the door behind him. The ripple effect of Mark Fredrick's death was spreading far and wide.

As Alex closed the door, he turned to see Christine glaring at him.

"What do you think you are doing?" she challenged him.

"I'm just trying to be nice Chris, give me a break. You're not the only one hurting here. We are all hurting."

Chris was the name he had always called her. To him, she wasn't Christine, she was Chris, it was his term of endearment. Ordinarily, she had hated her name being shortened, but with Alex it was different. When he said it, it caused her to feel wonderfully warm and loved. For her it was one of those special things that only a couple shares. Her mother Rose, had always insisted that as she had birthed her, and named her; if she had wanted her to be called Chris, she would have named her that herself. Everyone always told Rose that it would be shortened eventually once Christine was in school, but it never was, until Alex.

Christine looked at Alex and scowled.

"*Don't call me Chris.*" Her tone of voice, and what she said, took him by surprise and hurt him deeply.

"What?" Alex looked back at her, puzzled.

"My name is CHRISTINE, and no amount of praying will bring Mark back, not in Spain, not anywhere, so why don't you just piss off and enjoy the bloody cake if it's that important to you!"

Jessica, who was sitting on the stairs, silently observed for the first time ever her mother speaking to her father with such disdain. Once again she felt her world was spinning out of control but it was almost as though things had just shifted up a gear. Nothing had ever come between her mum and her dad before. They weren't like the other parents of many of her friends. Her parents' relationship was indestructible—or so she had believed. They were the couple that everyone else wished they could be; they had the perfect relationship that could survive all things. *All things except this*, thought Jessica as the now oh-so-familiar pangs of guilt washed over her. She silently got up and retreated to the safety of her bedroom.

Christine also retreated. She went directly to the kitchen and poured herself a large glass of red wine. It was three in the afternoon, and these days Christine was relying more and more on the calming effects she derived from alcohol to help settle her nerves. Wine helped her, she told herself as she threw yet another empty bottle into the recycle bin. The clink of glass on glass was an obvious reminder of the amount she had consumed in the last 48 hours, since the recycle bin had been emptied two days before.

The church group in Spain prayed for Mark and for his family. They prayed for people from across the globe that none of them would probably ever meet or know. They prayed for a mother and a father, they prayed for sisters, grandparents and friends who had lost a young man, snatched away from them long before he was meant to go. Most of all they prayed that everyone connected to this tragedy could find forgiveness and peace.

One of the parishioners was Sofia Rodriguez. She prayed hardest of all for a mother she did not know. She went home and placed a candle on an altar in her home. Above the altar was another candle, and a picture of another young man who had also taken his own life just ten years before: Alejandro Rodriguez, her son. She had carried her grief alone for many years and it was only her faith that had allowed her to carry on. Initially, as one might expect, her faith had been challenged, but she had an underlying belief that had carried her through. We all have been given free will, she thought. We all have the ability to make our own choices and create our own path. She eventually returned to the church, and when she did, they wrapped their loving arms around her, supporting her when she could not support herself. It was indescribably difficult during those early years. She, better than most, knew and understood the terrible pain and despair of losing a child.

As she lit the candle for Mark, she knelt down with tears in her eyes and prayed for a faceless woman across the globe. She prayed for her pain and she prayed for her grief as she embraced the understanding of an unseen sisterhood based on the maternal crippling grief they both now shared.

* * *

Mark had been observing it all. He had been on this journey with Grace by his side, able to witness all that had happened in the wake of his suicide. He looked on as the unknown woman knelt before the altar with tears in her eyes as the two candles burned in front of her. She seemed to be praying. She was speaking Spanish, but Mark somehow understood that she was praying for a boy. The picture of a young man caught his eye. He turned to Grace and asked who she was praying for. Grace just smiled and said, "You."

Mark looked confused.

"This is your ripple, Mark; it has already reached the other side of the world, and this is just one of the ripples we are seeing. There are so many more reaching out in every direction. This woman will continue to pray for you and your mother for years to come, because she understands. She too lost a son ten years ago. She too, knows the pain and horror of a mother losing her child.

* * *

Christine, who was completely unaware of all that was transpiring on the other side of the world, attempted to carry on some semblance of a life that she knew was never going to be normal again, a life that did not feel right in any way. In fact, she wondered just how it would *ever* be possible for her to carry on at all. To do so somehow felt like she was dishonouring Mark. *Should she just forget all about him and pretend he never existed? Should she just play happy families as if everything were ok? Is that what everyone expected of her?* She had no idea what was supposed to happen in such situations, but she knew she could never do that.

Secretly she continued to carry the weight of her guilt like a millstone around her neck that was threatening to drag her down into an abyss of the darkest depression. The ever-present weight of these thoughts and feelings were day by day getting harder for her to endure. *If only she had spoken up, if only she had torn herself away from her own misplaced priorities, if only...if only...if fucking only.*

She truly believed that Mark would still be alive *if only* she had taken action. She could have helped him, but now nothing could ever be ok again. She longed to be able to just go back in time, to have the opportunity to make different choices and in doing so, create a different outcome. But she could not. The feeling that she had failed them all was growing stronger with each passing day, and she could not discuss it with any of them.

Her mother was worried. She had tried to get Christine to talk about her feelings. They had always been so close and had always told each other everything. There had never been any topics that were off limits, until now.

Whenever Rose tried to get her daughter to talk about how she was coping or what she was thinking, Christine shut down the conversation, often changing the subject. The message was clear. Christine would not talk about Mark.

Rose was fighting her own battle as the matriarch of the family. She was desperately searching for ways to hold her struggling family together. She could see them all sinking into their own despair and there seemed nothing she could do to help. She herself was grieving the loss of her firstborn grandson. A precious, beautiful boy who had had such potential, but he was more than that to her. He was her Mark, her little Mark. The little boy she had nursed and nurtured as a baby. The little boy she had taken to the park, pushed on the swings and helped with his homework. The little Mark she had walked beside, supported through all his athletic successes as it took him around Australia, competing in national competitions. She had stood beside his parents, congratulating him alongside them, and celebrating all of his achievements. How was it that at his time of absolute need, she had been completely oblivious?

Born in 1950, Rose had seen a good many seasons come and go in her life. She had witnessed the ups and downs of a generation and she knew all about strength and resilience. God only knows she was a strong woman, but this was different. This was something she could not make better. She could find no silver lining, no purpose, no reason to all of this, simply because there *was* no reason. Her beautiful, talented and loving grandson had taken his own life. It made no sense at all.

However, Rose had no time to indulge herself in such thoughts. She needed to support her family. Her daughter and son-in-law were going through the worst time of their lives, and were having difficulty just getting through each day. She needed to be there for her grandchildren. How on earth could they ever deal with such an atrocity? Unspeakable trauma had been visited upon them in their own home, and the damage from what they had both witnessed could never be expunged. Rose needed to be strong for them all. She would save her own grieving for the quiet, private evening hours, when she felt free to cry softly into her pillow for her own momentous loss, as her life partner, her husband, silently held and comforted his ageing wife.

Christine's sister Samantha had been at the house nearly every day in the weeks following the funeral to help out with the running of the household in any way she could. She did the washing and helped make meals and ensured the girls and Alex were eating, while Christine often just sat lost in thought. Sam, unlike Christine, had always insisted that *her* name *should* be shortened; she was cool Aunty Sam. She too was grieving the monumental loss of her nephew, but she put her grief aside whenever she entered the Fredrick household; she needed to be there for the girls, she was especially worried about them.

Alex had returned to work. He seemed to have thrown himself into it as a form of coping with everything that was happening at home. Longer hours than usual, often six days a week, were occupying his time. He and Christine were now often snapping at each other whenever he *was* home. Christine had also taken to imbibing more and more wine *every* night. Something she had never done before was now becoming a habit.

Christine could feel herself becoming emotionally distant and less tolerant of everyone and everything. She believed the wine helped her to relax. It helped her to block out the terrible repetitive thoughts for brief periods of time, but as the weeks drew on she needed more. She knew it was not a healthy way to deal with her grief, but this felt in some way an added incentive for her. It was a form of self-sabotage and she was completely unaware of why she was doing it.

She had always striven to have such a fit and healthy body, but now, even though she did not recognise her own motives, the frequency of her drinking was, on a deeper level, serving the purpose of punishing herself for not being the mother she should have been. Perhaps all the focus she had placed on her own health and her own body had in some way contributed to her complete ignorance of what was going on in her son's life. She did not realise it at the time, but Christine was headed down a path of self-destruction which somehow made sense to her deeper mind. She did not deserve to be healthy when her son was dead.

One night a month or so later, when unusually Alex was *not* working, he asked her if she really needed to drink *again* this evening. This enraged Christine who was now like a different person; snappy, argumentative. "How dare you judge me!" she said. "You are never home anyway, why don't you just go back to work! You obviously prefer it there and I'm sure your pretty secretary will see to your every need, and give you *everything* you require. It seems you are not interested in getting much of *anything* here anymore."

Even as she said those words, she hated herself. She knew there was no foundation for them. She just wanted to lash out at him; she wanted to find his jugular and attack it, over and over again, until he hurt as much as she did. *Why had he not seen that his son was unwell? Why was he not to blame? Why did he just get to go on as normal when she couldn't?*

She hated him for that, and she hated herself for hating him.

She was in such conflict with herself these days, that she was ever so slowly becoming the woman she wanted him to hate. She didn't really understand why, but it seemed that she was unable to stop herself.

Jessica was, once again, sitting on the stairs listening to the now familiar bickering between her mother and father. She had never known her mother to drink so regularly or be so rude. She had also never heard her mother and father speaking to each other in such an uncaring way. It seemed to her that her mother was hell bent on creating an argument and her father was doing nothing to stop it. *Why* was he doing nothing to stop it? Didn't he realise that they were becoming just like all the other parents?

Was her father having an affair with his secretary? 'Please God, no!' Jessica thought.

Her parents had been so in love before all this happened.

This was her fault, she knew it; it was just another consequence of what she had allowed to happen in the first place. If she had not passed that bloody door on that bloody day; if only stupid Mark had told her what was going on—but no, he was a selfish pig. She was beginning to feel more and more antagonism toward the memory of her brother, who was no longer here to defend himself. *This really was all his fault. He caused all of this. How dare he do this to them all.* Jessica was as angry at him as she was at herself. *He doesn't have to deal with the consequences of his stupid actions. He doesn't have to see his whole world falling apart.* Her growing anger continued to mix with her grief and guilt such that she was not sure what she felt any more. Life was a mess, and now because of Mark, nothing would ever be the same again.

Jessica went upstairs to check on Hannah. She had been non-verbal since the news of Mr. Fryer's death compounded the trauma of what she had already seen on that terrible day. The psychologist said it was her way of coping, her way of desperately trying to maintain some sort of control in her life by shutting down and disassociating from the trauma. Hannah was in her bed turned away from the door with the covers pulled right up over her face. Jessica silently straightened the covers, tucked her in, and kissed her on the forehead before silently closing the door behind her. She made her way to her own bedroom, put on her headphones and allowed the loud music to drown out the sound of her own thoughts. She was aware that she had a science exam the next morning at school and had done no study at all, but she did not care. In fact, she wanted to fail, she felt guilty and although she did not readily recognise her motives, success does not sit well with guilt.

* * *

As Hannah heard footsteps approach her bedroom, she quickly pulled up the covers and closed her eyes pretending to be asleep. She gripped her teddy tightly. No words had come to her since news of the death of Mr. Fryer. It was not a choice to stop speaking, not something she actually decided to do or not to do: it just was. Hannah did not understand why it felt far more comforting for her to be silent, but it was almost as though words had just left her that day. She really did not think that she had any words left–she wasn't quite sure just where they may have gone, but they just weren't there anymore.

Christine and Alex had taken her to see the doctor to get a referral to a psychologist. The doctor told them that she was probably just trying to get attention, seeking comfort in some way because of all that had happened and he was sure she would be ok, but Hannah did not want attention. She would have been happy to retreat from the world all on her own. As long as she had her teddy, Pabby, and a colouring book, she did not have to think of Mark or that terrible day. She did not think of Mr. Fryer or that stupid surprise. She now hated surprises, but she did not think about that either. She did not think much at all. She was just living life in this moment. Doing what she was asked to do, eating when she was asked to eat, going to bed when she was asked to go to bed. She liked Jessica tucking her into bed, it felt nice, but she did not even speak to Jessica. To do anything else was too hard. To think anything else was too painful. To allow thoughts to penetrate this moment was too destructive, and so her thoughts had just shut down. She was living life in a protective void separate from the past. In this moment there was nothing scary happening. In this moment, she had her Pabby.

Hannah had not been back to school since the trauma of that terrible day back in March. Christine had taken her once, but she had just sat in class and stared at the board; she didn't talk, didn't play, didn't eat. The teacher had looked on concerned for this little girl who had endured so much. It was unsettling for the other children who didn't understand what was happening to their friend and classmate. Miss Langhorne knew that Hannah was not ready. She went into the staffroom and called Christine to pick her up. Unfortunately, Christine was in no fit state to do much at all that day, let alone pick up Hannah. She had begun drinking earlier than usual, so Jessica walked Hannah home and did not return.

11

ALEX: LIFE GOES ON

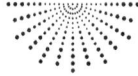

A lex looked at his wife and was again getting the feeling that he was looking at a stranger. Who was this woman who looked just like his beautiful wife, but who instead of being loving and gentle was actively hostile toward him? He was aware that she was grieving a loss that no parent should ever have to grieve, but so was he. He too was going through the most difficult time in his life, but for the first time in his marriage he felt completely unsupported; he felt completely alone. Of course he had the love and support of other family members who were all in their own way trying to make sense of this nonsensical tragedy, but that was different to the support only a spouse can give. Christine and Alex had always been able to talk about everything–why wouldn't she talk to him about this most important of issues?

Alex reflected on the trauma of the previous months. He had flash-backs about the phone call that had forever changed his life, and he had started having regular nightmares. The disturbing nightmares were so vivid and so realistic that Alex would often awaken in a cold sweat. The content of horror would vary from night to night, but the essence was always the same. Alex was unable to save Mark's life.

Often he dreamt that Mark was handing him a phone, and the more Alex reached for the phone the further it seemed to get away from him. Then Mark would vanish, leaving a disembodied phone floating always just out of Alex's reach. He could hear Mark's voice in the receiver, desperately calling to him:

"Dad...Dad...Help me, Dad...I need you DAD! Take the phone...why won't you take the phone? Why won't you help me...help me...I can't breathe."

The phone would develop wings and morph into an aeroplane and swiftly fly away out of sight, as Mark's voice would fade further and further into the distance until there was finally silence. Once the phone was gone, Alex was left desperately searching in anguish for Mark, never able to find him. Alex would often wake himself up, startled by his own thrashing around in the bed, his heart racing, his breathing rapid, as he cried out for his son in utter despair waking Christine as he did.

These night terrors heralded the cruel reality that the torment of losing his son did not end for Alex, whether his eyes were open or shut. For him there was to be no avoiding the horrific truth, even in his sleep. He desperately needed to find an escape from all the prompts and cues within his own home that continued to bombard his senses forever reminding him that his only son was dead. He needed to be away from his house and everything that it represented. Sadly, as much as it made his heart sink, in an attempt to deal with his own deep despair, he knew it was also necessary for him to put some distance between himself and the toxic person Christine was becoming. He had to keep busy, and work it seemed was his only escape.

Christine had been angry at first. She didn't understand how he could think clearly enough to function, let alone work, but, according to Alex, it was not up for discussion. He had called the Sydney office on the Friday after the funeral, when he could no longer stand being home.

Alex was a senior partner in the firm and currently ran the Melbourne office. There were six senior partners, one based in Melbourne, two in Queensland and three in Sydney at the head office, which housed opulent office suites overlooking the harbour. There were six junior partners and many paralegals and secretarial staff that were employed by the firm. All Senior Partners were answerable to the founding member based in Sydney. Stewart Huckett's reputation was synonymous with law reform in the country and he was well respected worldwide for his brilliant legal mind. Once you held the position of senior partner in Huckett & Associates you had job security assured for the rest of your legal career.

Mr. Huckett currently managed all of the international business and frequently travelled the world. It was he who had called the *in-person meeting* for all senior members on that fateful day when Alex had received the phone call that had turned his life upside down.

Alex Fredrick was Huckett's star employee, who some had speculated was in line to take over from the great man when the time came. He was the only one absent on the day of that all-important board meeting with no explanation as to why. Huckett had become concerned at Alex's absence. He checked his phone for the second time that morning when a text from Alex Fredrick finally lit up his screen.

It was only four words, but the message was clear.

Urgent

Flying home

Alex

Huckett had rubbed at his balding head and had handed his phone to his trusted secretary after receiving the message that morning. He said surreptitiously in a tone that conveyed *'do it now!'* "Find out what's going on, and don't discuss it with anyone until you have spoken to me."

It was unprecedented for Alex to be absent from a senior partner's meeting and Stewart Huckett had an uncanny instinct that had always served him well. He knew something was very wrong when his most trusted senior partner was not only on his way back home to Melbourne, but, even more out of character, he had failed to explain himself. This left a very uneasy feeling in the pit of Stewart Huckett's very ample belly.

The scheduled meeting at Huckett & Associates had gone ahead as planned, but not with the original agenda. Huckett did not disclose his reason for calling the meeting. He was a man who always played his cards close to his chest. Unbeknownst to anyone present, he had been about to make a major announcement that would impact them all; an announcement that was directly related to Alex Fredrick.

Patricia, the indispensable, trusted secretary and personal assistant to Mr. Huckett had set to work. Naturally, Alex was not answering his phone, so she called Alex's wife Christine Fredrick. Due to the often-sensitive nature of work done by the firm, as a senior partner it was essential that Alex be contactable at all times. The remuneration for such an infrequently required intrusion was well worth it. Thus, the firm kept a very detailed and up-to-date file on all senior partners' contact details, and those of all next of kin, including parents and children. It had proven to be extremely useful on more than one occasion, and, again, it was invaluable today.

Christine Fredrick did not answer her phone. At the time, she had collapsed on the floor in the Emergency Department's waiting room, unable to think and totally unable to comprehend the unspeakable insanity of what had just happened to her first-born child.

Patricia had scanned through the contact list deciding whom to call next. She chose Alex's mother. The phone had rung only one time before an apprehensive Mary Fredrick answered in a concerned tone.

Two minutes later Patricia had hung up the phone. She then knocked on the boardroom door and interrupted the senior partners' meeting, an intrusion only she could get away with. She went directly to Stewart Huckett and whispered something discreetly in his ear, then quickly turned and left.

His expression, in front of the entire boardroom and all the senior partners, had been indecipherable.

* * *

Stewart Huckett was happy to hear that Alex was finally returning to work to run the Melbourne office. Huckett's personal way of dealing with such trauma, was not to deal with it at all. He was a strong believer in submerging yourself in work and all would be well, eventually. Life has a way of sorting itself out, he often mused, and this was his personal ethos.

"Keep yourself busy, son," was his only advice, and that is exactly what Alex intended to do.

Christine, on the other hand, had taken an indefinite leave of absence from her work at the real estate agency. She was having trouble just getting out of bed in the morning. The thought of putting on a happy face and pretending that she actually cared about the dollar value some arrogant vendor put on a property, or pretending that everything was all right in her life was abhorrent to her and something she could not even contemplate.

She didn't know if she could return to a normal life ever again. How could she be expected to function at work when clearly she could not even cope at home? She held herself directly responsible for Mark's death and for her inability to recognise what was happening under her own roof. To return to work seemed unconscionable. She harboured a growing feeling of resentment toward Alex for his apparent ability to just move on with his life. So, she continued to find her own comfort where she could by losing herself in several glasses of wine each night to take the edge off her sadness.

One evening as Christine poured herself yet another glass of wine, which on this particular occasion signalled the consumption of the entire bottle before 7pm, Alex became even more concerned; this behaviour was now becoming the usual instead of the exception. Christine was aware that Alex was watching her, and felt he was also judging her. She did not care, in fact she resented him for it.

Alex had been watching his beautiful wife slipping down a rabbit hole and he felt he could do nothing to help. She was slowly becoming unrecognisable. But Alex was not in the habit of 'doing nothing.' When there was a problem, he would always seek a solution. He took a deep breath as he slowly and deliberately considered his words before he spoke. He turned to Christine, ready to broach the subject.

"Honey, " he began in his softest voice, "I think you've been hitting the wine a bit hard. Do you think we would benefit from some counselling?" He had truly hoped this could be the answer they both needed.

Hearing those words from Alex confirmed what she was desperately trying to ignore. She was not yet ready to accept the truth, so she flung her full glass of red wine in his general direction and stumbled angrily towards the stairs. God, she *was* angry! She was hurting and she was in no mood to talk to him or a bloody counsellor. *What the hell could they do? Bring Mark back from the dead?*

Then she really let loose as words she would later regret flowed like a vile tirade from her mouth.

"You're such an asshole, Alex.

Do you even care that our son is *dead,* or is your work more important? Fuck off with your bloody counselling, perhaps *you* need counselling to start feeling something!"

As she mounted the stairs, she shot one parting comment in his general direction. "And if I *want* a bloody drink, I'll have a bloody drink, so you can all just fuck off!"

Christine went upstairs, allowing the self-loathing thoughts to consume her. She hated herself for what she had just said, but she didn't know how to stop. She threw herself on the bed in her un-showered, unruly state, teeth and hair unbrushed, and allowed the alcohol to do its job. Almost instantly she slipped into a drunken deep sleep that would last only a few hours. It was almost as though her body was participating in a sick kind of conspiracy, deliberately trying to taunt her further. Sleep would then abandon her, and she would awaken in the early hours only to be forced to lie awake and further endure her pain and torment.

* * *

Jessica, who was aware her mother had emotionally deserted both herself and her sister, had taken up the role of being Hannah's carer. Hannah, more than anyone, needed support right now. Jessica had no idea how much she was suffering, or even the emotional impacts of such tragedy on a young mind, but what she did know was that her little sister had emotionally disappeared. The Hannah of old was no longer recognisable. So much change in a few short weeks, and Jessica wondered how long this would last, or if she would ever see her little sister again. She knew she needed to be there for her and to take care of her. There was a synergy in her actions; it was as impor-tant for Jessica to give this support as it was for Hannah to receive it. The very act of giving and receiving this care and support seemed to strengthen the allegiance between the two.

The grandparents and the aunts and uncles had all been around a lot in the early weeks. In fact, there was always someone around in the beginning, but as the weeks became months their presence was noticeably diminishing. They all had their own lives to get on with, and the Fredricks had theirs. Jessica felt it was as though they were all just supposed to stop talking about Mark and move on, and so she did. However, it was one thing to stop talking about him, but quite another to stop thinking about him. The truth was, she could not stop thinking about what she had witnessed on that terrible day.

These thoughts were disturbing her sleep and impacting on her daylight hours. She had been sick almost constantly since Mark's death. A cold had turned into a chest infection that she could not shift, followed by an ear infection and cold sores. Nanna Rose had taken her to the doctor for antibiotics which still lay unopened on the bedroom floor. Jessica did not care that she was sick. She didn't care about anything, except Hannah, who just seemed to be going through the motions of existing. Jessica wondered if anyone else in the house was concerned about her too, but it did not seem so.

Grandma Mary came around on Wednesdays in her red Toyota Corolla. Her twenty-year-old 'little gem,' as she called it, allegedly had the most wonderful fuel economy. How would she actually know, Jessica had often pondered, as it truly was the quintessential granny's car, literally only driven to church on Sundays. Now the 'little gem' had another regular appointment. As Jessica's mother was incapable of doing much at all these days, Grandma Mary had been tasked with Hannah's weekly psychology visits.

To begin with, Jessica would ask her grandmother how things had gone, but the answer was always the same. A negative shake of the head now indicated that Hannah continued to maintain her silence. As the weeks marched on, the appointments became less frequent. It seemed there was nothing much that could be done for Hannah. Initially, Hannah had listened to the psychologist going over the events of that day and the days that followed, explaining things in terms that Hannah could understand. Hannah actually did not *want* to understand, and always sat expressionless, silently holding her teddy and waiting for the fifty-minute session to be over. When the time was up she obediently left the room and headed for the car.

They were told that there was nothing physical that could be fixed or healed with a magic tablet; it really was just a waiting game. The psychologist said that Hannah had become silent when the trauma of what she had witnessed in her brother's room was compounded by the death of her beloved friend. It had all become too much for her to bear. Her place of safety had instantly become unsafe, and she did not possess the tools to deal with such disturbingly traumatic experiences.

One day, when Hannah felt safe, she would speak again. The psychologist had told them so, but, until then, Jessica would care for her needs. The two sisters shared a bond now, connected by this terrible mutual experience; one through innocence, one through guilt.

* * *

Over the months that followed, Alex and Christine, both grieving the loss of their son in their own way, continued to drift further and further apart. Neither did much to prevent this from happening. There was a mutual disdain that was developing within them and it was growing stronger by the day, as neither one of them could, or would, understand the other. Christine could not understand how Alex was apparently getting on with his life as though nothing had happened, and Alex could not understand how Christine had seemed to have completely given up on hers.

The arguments and snide comments added to the already unhealthy atmosphere that now permeated through the Fredrick household. Happiness and laughter had long since left, and in its place, a depressing emptiness lingered, tainted by the now frequent smell of alcohol and the copious stack of Christine's empty bottles. It was certainly a depressing place, and, as much as it pained Alex to leave his daughters, he felt he just couldn't be there. He knew he was running away by burying himself in his work as he spent more and more time at the office. He was aware this was more by choice than necessity, but he did it anyway.

The managing director, Stewart Huckett, had encouraged Alex to return to work to keep busy and Alex was pleased he had listened. Home was becoming somewhere he did not want to be. Huckett had flown down for the funeral of Mark Fredrick. He was a man of many contradictions. Family first, he had told Alex. "Do what you need to do, but get back to work as soon as you can. It's better that way, for everyone."

Now Stewart Huckett had an announcement to make. The very announcement he had wanted to make that fateful day. This time he did not call a meeting. He had made up his mind; there would be no discussion with the firm's other partners. They would be told once the decision had been made and the position had been accepted, as he knew it would be. Huckett was very used to getting his own way.

The phone call from Stewart Huckett came through at 8:30 am on Friday morning. Alex had been summoned to the head office for a meeting with Huckett, alone. The other partners were not to be in attendance.

"I'm not going to mess around, my boy, " Huckett said.

"I think we both know why I'm calling you up here. It's time for you to start thinking about your future in the company. I'm not going to be doing all the international travel next year. I want to groom you to fill in many of my responsibilities. I think we both know what this means, where this leads, Alex. I have chosen you as the probable successor to lead the company when I step away. That's not happening just yet though, so don't get too excited, all in good time my boy. You're not getting rid of this old pain in the ass that easily. I do want to see you though, face to face— so we can begin to discuss a timeline for your transition. Assuming, as I am, that you are accepting my very generous and sought-after offer. No need to answer that, it was a rhetorical question. Of course you'll be accepting my offer. I'll be seeing you on Monday morning at nine sharp," he directed, then promptly hung up.

Alex stood there with the phone still in his hand, his mouth open as if about to say something. He could not believe what he had just heard. He, Alex Fredrick, was to lead one of the most prestigious law firms in the country. It was a dream come true. There were others who may not have shared Huckett's sentiments, but at the end of the day, nobody ever argued with Stewart Huckett.

Alex put down the phone and his first and immediate instinct was to call Christine; his wife, his lover, his confidant, but he resisted the urge. Christine was not the Christine of old any more. This called for a celebration of the greatest proportions, but he would have given it up in a millisecond if it had meant having his son back. He knew that was impossible. In reality, this was a small glimmer of light in the darkness, the first promise of life beyond losing Mark.

Alex did not want to live life without his son, but one fact remained; he needed to go on. The rest of his family depended upon it. Hannah and Jessica needed a father, and he would not let them down. As painful as it was, he needed to allow life to begin again. He would tell Christine when he got home. For the first time in months there was some good news, something to look forward to. He didn't want this moment sullied by what he believed Christine might say. He instead picked up the phone and booked his early Monday morning flight to Sydney. When this was done, he called his father to share the news with him.

"Hi Dad," Alex said quietly as a tear gently escaped him. "I have some news I want to tell you."

'Bobby' as he was affectionately known by many, waited patiently for his son to compose himself.

"You okay, Son?" came his compassionate reply.

The sound of his father's voice seemed to open an emotional flood gate, and all that Alex had suppressed began to well up from deep inside of him. Months of pain and anguish slowly released, seeping out of him uncontrollably, directly into the safety of his father's confidence.

Alex knew his father could cope with anything he had to say; in fact, Bob had been waiting for his son to come to him when the time was right. He already knew there was trouble in Alex's marriage. His own beloved wife, Mary Fredrick, was one of the most astute women he knew, and had told him on the day of the funeral that they were headed for trouble. She had noticed it; the usually strong bond between husband and wife was tenuous even then, but Bob hadn't realised just how bad things had become. Alex spared no details. He told his father everything. For Alex the relief of speaking to his father was palpable. The thoughts and feelings that he had held within now flowed freely and it felt good to let it all out. Alex told his father about the promotion and how bitter sweet it was. They spoke for an hour about Mark, about the girls, and eventually about Christine.

Alex had not spoken about his relationship with anyone until this moment. To do so he felt would have been a betrayal, but now he needed help. His every fear and concern came flooding out. He told his father how he was afraid he was losing his wife and feared there was nothing he could do to prevent it. He felt as though she was drowning in a sea of grief that was slowly but surely dragging her under, and, as hard as he tried to save her, he could feel her limp hand slipping out of his grasp. For her part, Christine was doing nothing to prevent the inevitable devastation. He feared what might happen when she was finally adrift, all alone in the darkness and despair with nothing to keep her afloat.

Alex knew he could say anything to his father, and he did. He told him everything. Bob listened patiently. When he had said everything he needed to release, his father said "I'm so sorry Alex, this must all be so difficult. I really don't know what to do for you, except to be here—day or night I'm here for you."

"I know dad."

"I haven't told her about the promotion. I don't know how to. She will be angry. She hates it that I have gone back to work. She feels that I'm not hurting and that I have just gone on with my life. But I *am* hurting, Dad—and it hurts so bloody much I can hardly breathe. I just don't know what else to do. Work is somehow easier than being at home, because I'm not surrounded by the constant reminders of what I have lost. My son, my beautiful boy, and now—now my wife."

Tears began to flow freely now and it felt right. He had held it all in for so long, but here in the safety and sanctity of his father's confidence, Alex could finally let go.

12

THE PROMOTION

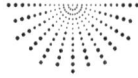

Alex arrived home that Friday evening at 8 o'clock. A part of him felt relief after speaking with his father, but there was another part of him that felt anxious about confronting Christine with this news; at any other time, this would have been a great cause for celebration. He really did not want to come home at all anymore, but today, this feeling was compounded by the fact he was beginning to resent Christine for her inability to move forward with him. What other choice did they have? Their lives would go on one way or another, with or without Mark. The thought of this made him want to die; but he would *not* die. He would go on without his beloved son because that is what happens in the real world, you just have to go on. His daughters' future happiness depended on it.

He knew his wife needed help, but for some inexplicable reason he could not fathom, she would not accept help from anyone. She seemed to be welcoming her grief almost as though she *wanted* to feel bad. Her behaviours were incomprehensible. Alex was now exhausted by the constancy of trying to deal with his own grief, as well as that of the rest of his family, but he had grown so weary of Christine's aggression and indulgences that he wondered if he even possessed the resilience required to exist in this household any longer. Until today he had not wanted to acknowledge these thoughts, even to himself; to do so would surely mean that his marriage was heading in a direction he would never have believed was even possible.

Alex walked into the kitchen and found Christine sitting in silence at the breakfast bar. There was a broken wine glass on the floor surrounded by spilled wine remnants. The wine bottle sat empty on the bench top. Alex stared at his wife. Her hair was unbrushed, her clothes crumpled; he suspected that she had not showered in days and his heart ached for the wife he was losing more and more with each passing day. He had lost enough already.

"Christine, you need to get some help," he whispered despondently.

He was not up for another argument today. He left her there in silence and went upstairs to see his girls.

Hannah was already tucked up in bed asleep, or so he thought. He leaned over and kissed her on the forehead. He whispered to her softly, "Daddy's here. I love you beautiful girl. I love you so much. Everything will be all right. Sleep tight, my darling."

He adjusted her covers and delivered one final kiss to her little forehead then he slipped out of her room to go to see Jessica.

Hannah's eyes opened to the pale orange glow from the salt-lamp that illuminated her room and she watched as her father disappeared from view. A single tear escaped as she heard the gentle click of the door closing behind him.

Jessica was sitting on her bed with her head phones over her ears. She did not hear Alex knock and was unaware of his presence. As he stood and observed his eldest daughter, he could see the strain of the last months noticeable on her visibly thin face. There was a sadness about her that he could feel. She had been through so much, too much; more than any fifteen year old should ever have to endure. Not

134

only had she witnessed an atrocity, which would forever after permeate her young mind and steal her innocence, she was now also dealing with a family that was falling apart. She had a mother who could not cope, a father who was distant, and a sister so traumatised that she had sunk into her own silent world to escape it all.

Yes, Jessica was enduring a great deal, but Alex did not know the whole truth. He did not know that the major thing his daughter was desperately trying to deal with was the very same thing that was crippling his wife and threatening his marriage. A guilt so intense, so debilitating and so insidious that it was threatening to sink them both.

Alex called his daughters name. Jessica opened her eyes and looked at her father standing in her room.

"Hi Dad," she said

"Hi," he smiled, "Can I sit down?"

"Sure."

He sat and held her hand, enjoying her touch and the peaceful silence that surrounded them. Here at least in this moment he could relax.

"You okay?" she asked.

"Yeah...how's Hannah?"

"She's okay, just the same, except she smiled at Benny today, so that's good isn't it?"

"Yes, that's great," he said.

"Jess, I have some news..."

Jessica looked on expectantly.

Alex went on to tell his daughter about the promotion and what that would mean for the whole family. He said that it would mean additional money, which would be great, and extra responsibility, but also it would mean that he would be away from home a lot more. There was a part of him that was very aware that this was probably the last thing his daughter wanted to hear right at this critical time in their lives, and perhaps it was the last thing he should be considering right now—but it was the only way forward for him. He too was drowning, and this was his lifeline. This was his way to pull himself back to shore. He truly hoped his daughter would understand.

"What do you think, Jess?" he asked tentatively. "I won't do it if you don't want me to."

He prayed his daughter would agree.

"That's great, Dad, it will be good for you—" Jessica said with forced enthusiasm. She managed a smile as she put her headphones back on, fighting back the tears. She closed her eyes.

Can things get any worse? she wondered.

Alex stood and left his daughter's room. He was aware that he had no way of knowing if Jessica was speaking the truth or just saying what she knew he wanted to hear. Perhaps he really should have known the obvious answer, but he did not question her response. His mind was made up. He had not even spoken to Christine yet, but he was going to Sydney on Monday morning to accept the promotion of a lifetime. How could he not?

On Saturday morning Alex told Christine the news. He thought that the morning was the safest time to speak with her. She appeared to have a hangover. This was now a regular occurrence, but today it could possibly work in his favour. She probably would not yell with a raging headache, but more importantly her mind was clear of alcohol at this time of the day, and so there was the slightest possibility that he actually may find 'Christine.' He knew she was in there some-where, deeply buried within the facade of this stranger in front of him, who was so very badly attempting to impersonate his beautiful wife.

Christine took the news better than expected, which in itself was surprising. She did not congratulate him however; in fact, she did not comment at all. She didn't express an opinion, good or bad. She didn't argue or yell, she just silently nodded her head and eventually said 'fine,' and left the room.

"Fine," Alex repeated to himself as he let out a despondent sigh. "Fine." Except, nothing was fine.

Alex had gone in to the office on Saturday to escape the house, but he had made a concerted effort to spend Sunday with the girls. He took them both to the pictures and then to the beach park for ice-cream and a walk. Hannah silently ate hers while Jessica was noticeably distant. She deliberately dropped her ice-cream on the ground, pretending it was an accident, but in reality she was eating less and less as the weeks passed and nobody seemed to notice, which served her well. She did not want to play 'happy families' anymore. She was there for one reason and one reason only; she was there for Hannah. Alex sat on the park bench watching his daughters, and he felt his heart sink at the sight of what his family had become.

He had pinned his hopes on this new opportunity. He hoped it would be their way out of the despair; something good for them to look forward to, but in reality, he was beginning to realise that the only person who was thinking this was him. He pushed these thoughts away as he walked toward the beach on his own. The girls did not follow him. He stared out to sea and wondered what was to become of his beloved family.

* * *

Alex woke early on Monday morning before the alarm went off. It was 4:44am. Christine was finally asleep beside him after yet another disturbed night. He reached across to turn off his alarm before it sounded and woke her. He reset it for 7:15am, so that Christine could get up and get Jessica ready for school. Even as he did this he knew that she would probably *not* get up. She would probably turn the alarm off and pull the blankets over her head and retreat back into the warmth and darkness of the bed covers. This was becoming the norm, but, ever hopeful, he turned it on anyway. In reality he knew that it would be Jessica who would get herself ready for school, and Nanna Rose who would drive by the house to ensure she got to school on time.

Rose was becoming very concerned about the decline she could see in her youngest daughter. She had called Cathy, Christine's best friend, on several occasions to see if together they could find answers to help the woman they both loved; but they had no success. Christine seemed hell bent on continuing down this path of self-destruction and neither of these two women could understand why. Her son had died, and this was unimaginable; but she was systematically destroying all that she had left. They tried to understand what she must be enduring, but it was not possible.

They could not understand the guilt she held in her heart for the responsibility of this horrendous event. They could not fathom the depths of shame she felt, thinking she had failed as a mother. They didn't know that she blamed herself for her own selfish pursuits, believing that had cost the life of her son, and they would never understand how it felt so wrong to still be alive when her son was dead. They didn't know any of it. How could they ever, ever understand?

Everyone was suffering since the death of Mark, not least of all themselves in their own ways, but neither could reach Christine. She was enduring her own kind of hell, and there seemed no way for them to release her from that prison where only she held the key.

Alex took one last look at his sleeping wife and then selected his Yves Saint Laurent classic fit, single-breasted, black suit jacket from the robe and made his way to the downstairs bathroom to ready himself for the important day ahead. The jacket was part of a suit that Christine had bought him as a gift, and though it was an indulgence that was far more expensive than they could afford at the time, Christine had told him that it was symbolic of good things to come. He smiled as he reminisced about a happier time, a time when she had been so excited to give him this extravagant gift. Now, sadly, that felt like a lifetime ago.

After he showered, he slipped on his new white shirt, crisp and perfectly pressed, fresh from the dry cleaners. He always liked the smell of a freshly laundered shirt. There was something so comforting about it. It reminded him of his youth. He thought of the countless hours Mary Fredrick had spent standing at the ironing board ensuring all her boys were well presented.

"Don't think you are going out of this house looking like that, Alexander Fredrick!" she would say if she caught him escaping the house in yesterday's clothes.

"I won't have any of you going out and looking like you have no home, go and get changed this minute."

Again, Alex smiled at the memory. The truth was, yesterday's clothes were often perfectly clean and acceptable, but this was Mary's special way of looking after her family. She would have it no other way, and although they used to grumble at the inconvenience, neither would they.

He now had ten minutes to say goodbye to the girls and grab his things. The taxi was booked for 5:30 am to get him to the airport by 6:30 at the latest, allowing for traffic. He had already checked in online and would have time to go to the business lounge for a quick bite and a freshly brewed coffee before his flight.

Alex could see the yellow cab approaching their house from Jessica's bedroom window. "See you, Jess," he said.

"Good luck dad," came her sleepy reply.

Alex had instructed the taxi not to beep as he didn't want the neighbours to be disturbed. He quietly grabbed his briefcase and exited the house taking one last look up the stairs towards his bedroom. He had never before left for the airport without saying goodbye to his wife. So many things had changed.

He was greeted by the driver, a familiar face. "Morning Mr. Fredrick, off to the airport?"

"Thank you."

"Traffic's good this morning, so there should be no hold ups."

"That's great," said Alex. He put in his headphones to signal that he really did not wish to engage in small talk today. He had a lot to think about. He wasn't exactly sure how the meeting would pan out, but he was excited to finally have something to look forward to.

As he sat in the taxi, lost in thought about the last time he took this journey, Alex felt an unfamiliar pang in his stomach. Perhaps it was hunger, he really should have had some breakfast; he would get some when he arrived. The journey was fairly uneventful, the Monash freeway was flowing well, which was a pleasant surprise for this time of the morning. Alex sat back, closed his eyes and tried not to think.

The taxi arrived right on time. Tullamarine was already bustling with Monday morning commuters, many of whom were on their way to Sydney. He checked his digital boarding pass and made his way to the business lounge for breakfast. The feeling in his stomach was worsening.

He grabbed a coffee and some fruit toast with mascarpone cheese. It was comforting just to sit and wait. This was the part he normally liked the best; once he arrived he could relax and read the paper, but not today.

The fruit toast had not eased the feeling in his stomach; in fact, it was getting worse. By the time he was due to board the plane he was feeling hot. He wondered for a moment if he were coming down with something. His flight had been called. He did not feel well but he left the business lounge and made his way to the boarding gate. As he reached the gate lounge he must have looked as bad as he felt, because a steward asked him if he was okay.

"You are very pale sir. I think you need to take a seat."

"Yes, I think I will for a moment, thank you." He said as he looked for the nearest seat and immediately sat down.

As Alex sat his heart began to race; he was sweaty and feeling faint. He had an overwhelming feeling that he might die.

"I think I'm having a heart attack," Alex managed to get out right before his world began to spin and he found himself on the floor.

Attendants ran from every direction and someone called an ambulance. The airport doctor was called as Alex felt the pain in his chest getting stronger; he felt completely out of control. He was beginning to panic now. How could he be having a heart attack? He was too young, too healthy.

Shit...please, God, no...oh my god, am I having a heart attack...am I going to die?

Someone placed an oxygen mask on Alex's face, which felt intolerable because he could not breathe. He tried to take it off but the attending doctor replaced it. Alex had a cannula inserted into his vein to allow for intravenous access, His Yves Saint Laurent jacket had been thrown on the floor. Several droplets of red blood were a stark contrast against the crisp white of his shirt. Alex did not notice. He was placed on a gurney and a cardiac monitor was applied to his chest as he was wheeled away from the gate lounge to a private corner to wait for the ambulance. His blood pressure and pulse were off the scale and his hands and feet were feeling numb.

"God, this can't be happening."

The plane doors closed and the 7:15 flight to Sydney took to the air; it was fifteen minutes late, and it was without Alex Fredrick.

The ambulance paramedics arrived. They were so confident and reassuring.

"Hey Alex, I'm Simon and this is Joanne—we are going to look after you today, okay?"

Alex nodded weakly.

"We are just going to check a few things and get you comfortable, then we'll be taking you to St. Vincent's hospital for a full cardiac work up. Sound good?"

Mask in place, Alex was doing very little talking. He raised his thumb to signal okay.

They stabilised him and told him that his heart monitor tracing looked fine at the moment and his blood pressure and pulse were returning to normal.

Alex still had the heaviness in his chest and a sense of general unease, but he was feeling safer now that the paramedics seemed to be less concerned.

"Is there anyone we can call for you?" Simon asked.

Alex reached for his phone, unlocked it and searched for the number.

He handed it to Simon and pointed to the screen.

Bob picked up the call on the third ring. "Alex?" he sounded surprised. "Thought you would be on a plane by now?"

"Hello Mr Fredrick, this is Simon Harrison speaking. I'm a paramedic, I'm here with Alex, he is okay. He had some chest pain so we are taking him to St. Vincent's Hospital. We should be there in around thirty minutes. You can come in if you want to see how he is. He is stable at the moment, so no need to rush."

"*What?*" said his father, unable to comprehend what he had just heard. Without waiting for further explanation he said, "Yes, we will come straight in. Thank you."

He hung up the phone and quickly went to find Mary.

Mary sprang into action as she always did. She called Christine's mother, Rose, and asked if she could go to the house to tell Christine and the girls what was happening.

"The paramedics said he is stable, so we don't need to worry the girls with too much detail at this point," she stressed.

"I'm sure Christine will want to come in," she said, but even as the words left her mouth she realised that she really wasn't sure at all if this was true.

"I'm going to the hospital now with Bobby, I'll call you as soon as we know anything." Then she was gone.

Rose couldn't believe what she had just been told. It made no sense. Alex was one of the healthiest men she knew. How could it be possible that he may be having a heart attack? How much more could this family endure?

* * *

Mark watched on in the chaos of the airport gate lounge, not sure of exactly what was happening to his father in that moment, yet he somehow felt responsible. Was this his fault? Was this another of his ripples? If only he could comfort his father. If only he could let him know he was not alone. If only his father knew that Mark was right here with him.

Mark looked toward Grace. He was once again comforted and reassured by her presence. She simply smiled her divine heavenly smile toward him, then redirected her attention to the unfolding scene before them both.

* * *

Stewart Huckett sat in his office. It was five minutes past nine. Alex was five minutes late. Again.

Perhaps he had been caught in traffic, but if that was the case why had he not called to let the office know? This was out of character for Alex Fredrick. Huckett did not like 'out of character' scenarios; he also didn't like 'unexpected surprises.' If his star employee had not attended the head office for this significant meeting a second time, there had to be something very wrong. He called Alex's phone, which by now had been switched off and placed in the clothing bag beneath Alex's gurney, in the St. Vincent's Accident and Emergency department. Huckett, who was unaccustomed to being kept in the dark, especially by his most senior partner, called his secretary, the indispensable Patricia, and once again asked her to find out what the hell was going on.

As before, it was once again Mary Fredrick who first answered the phone. She was at the hospital with her husband. The details were still sketchy, but the long and the short of it was that Alex had been taken from Melbourne airport by ambulance to St. Vincent's Hospital with a suspected heart attack.

Patricia knocked on Stewart Huckett's door, "Excuse me, Sir," she said as she entered the office to explain the situation.

The expression on Stewart Huckett's face was indiscernible. He instructed Patricia to cancel his next appointment.

* * *

Alex had been moved to the Cardiac Care Unit by the time the doctor came to Alex's cubicle to explain the findings of the blood results and the cardiac monitoring.

"Everything has come back normal," the doctor said.

"That's great!" said Bob.

"Well, what happened to me then?" Alex asked incredulously.

"Something certainly happened. We think you may have had a panic attack, Alex. It's quite common. You can actually feel like you are having a heart attack. You can even feel as though you are dying," Dr. Nguyen explained. He was the A&E cardiac registrar on call for the day.

"What?" Alex said. "I wasn't panicked about anything. I was just about to catch a flight; I've done it thousands of times."

Dr. Nguyen had been informed of Alex's recent family trauma. It was part of the medical history to find out any major stressors that may be contributing to the possibility of potential cardiac issues.

"Can I ask you something, Alex?" said Dr. Nguyen gently.

"Of course."

"When was the last time you flew?"

"It was the day M..." he paused as the implications of that statement dawned upon him.

"Do you think that has something to do with today, Doctor?"

"I do, Alex. I would like to write you a referral to see one of my colleagues. She is a very experienced psychologist who works with a lot of post-traumatic stress cases just like this."

The words 'post-traumatic stress' rang in Alex's ears. He had experienced trauma, there was no denying it, but P.T.S.D. was something else, surely. If this were true, what would it mean for him? His mind raced. Would he ever fly again? What if he couldn't, and how would he ever explain this to Huckett? He would never understand P.T.S.D. as an excuse, but after today, Alex knew that this was not an excuse. He *never* wished to experience what he had been through today ever again.

Oh holy shit! Huckett! Alex suddenly remembered the meeting, and that he had once again stood his boss up. Nobody stood Stewart Huckett up twice... *Jesus!*

* * *

Stewart Huckett sat in stunned silence, leaning on his highly polished 19th Century French mahogany desk which he had imported directly from Paris two years ago. He was trying to process the bizarre information he had just received. He was not accustomed to making errors in judgment, but it seemed to him that this was exactly what he had inadvertently done. As thoughts rapidly flew through his sharp and somewhat narcissistic mind, he was quick to perceive the possible implications. He may have been imprudent to make such a hasty decision, he thought. He had not built this business on compassion, or on being liked. He realised he might need to reconsider his proposal to Alex. He would never allow all of his hard work to be lost by handing the reins over to someone who was not physically or emotionally up to the task, and although he would not put it quite like that to Alex, he knew Alex had now become a definite liability.

13

THE PSYCHOLOGICAL TOLL
CONTINUES

N anna Rose, appeared unconcerned, on the outside at least, as
she put on a happy face and entered the Fredrick household
that Monday morning after she had received the phone call that had
rocked her world once again. Her son-in-law had experienced a probable heart attack. The news was incomprehensible. *'What next?'* She
thought.

She did not tell the girls that their father had been taken to hospital
with a suspected heart attack. She thought it best to wait until they
had something definite to tell them. They had both endured enough
over the last months, and she didn't want to unduly worry them until
she knew there was something to worry about.

"Have you girls both had breakfast?" she asked.

The girls were now used to getting themselves up and ready for
the day.

Jessica had helped Hannah to get dressed and had made her some
toast. She had not eaten herself. She was now in the habit of missing
meals, and still, it had not been noted by anyone. After all, no one
was looking. It felt good for her to feel the pain of hunger, it was

somehow fitting. A punishment of sorts, and in a world that was spinning out of control for her, although she did not realise it herself, this was one thing she *could* control, and nobody had to know.

"Yes, Nanna, we've eaten," she lied.

"You are looking thin, Jess," Nanna said. "You need to eat more, love."

"I'm *fine,* Nan," she lied again.

Rose then made her daughter a cup of tea and headed upstairs. She knocked on the bedroom door; silence. She knocked again.

"Christine—it's mum,"

A sleepy groan was audible from inside the room.

"I'm coming in," said Rose.

Rose entered the room and saw Christine desperately trying to ignore the intrusion. She pulled the covers over her head and rolled away from her mother.

"Christine, I need to speak to you," her mother said in an assertive voice.

"Listen to me, *please.*"

Christine rolled back over and looked at her mother.

"What are you doing here? she asked as she took the cup of tea from her mother's hands.

"It's Alex."

"Alex is in Sydney."

"No Christine, he isn't."

Rose went on to describe what had happened at the airport, and to explain that Alex had been taken to St. Vincent's hospital in an ambulance. She said he was stable, but was awaiting the results of his assessment.

"The girls don't know; I haven't told them," she said. "I thought it was better that way."

Christine, despite still feeling slightly groggy from just being woken up, but mostly from the ill effects of the alcohol she had consumed the night before, felt fear grip her.

"Alex?" she asked, frightened.

"He's in Sydney. This can't be right, he's forty-eight years old for God's sake. Forty-eight year olds don't have heart attacks."

"Let's go to the hospital Christine, he needs you."

"No he doesn't, mum. He doesn't need anyone, just his work. That's quite ironic don't you think?"

"That's enough, Christine Fredrick," Rose snapped assertively.

"Get yourself up right now. I'll be downstairs with your daughters doing what *you* should be doing. It's time you started pulling yourself together Christine, if you want to save what's left of your *family*."

As the words left her mouth, a part of her immediately regretted them, but there was another part that knew it had to be said.

"I'm sorry, Christine, really I am—I shouldn't have said that. Just get dressed, *please*."

Rose left the room and stood in the hallway. She raised her hands to her head and covered her face. She had never wanted to cry more than she did at this very moment, but she could not. She would never worry her two precious granddaughters by letting them see her upset. She was not accustomed to raising her voice to her daughter, but she was beginning to feel so desperate, so helpless. It felt as though there was nothing she could do to prevent her daughter slowly disappearing before her very eyes, and the tattered remnants of her family vanishing with her. It was time to take action. Enough was enough. If Christine refused to seek help herself, Rose would help her, whether she wanted help or not.

Rose took a few moments to compose herself. She slipped into the bathroom to splash water on her face, ensuring it did not betray her emotions. She then went down stairs to check on the girls.

"Hurry up you two, let's get moving," she said in a bright tone.

Hannah continued to exist within her world of silence, and as such was still not going to school. The teacher was sending home some reading to do, but Nanna Rose still insisted she get up and ready for the day. Jessica was now ready and Rose would drive her, but first she needed to touch base with the hospital to see how things were going. She had to know what to say to Jessica.

Rose slipped into the back room and quietly called Mary Fredrick at the hospital.

"He's all right," Mary had said.

"The doctor has just left and they are discharging him."

"Discharging him? Was it his heart?" asked Rose.

"No," she paused, "They say it was..." She paused again, not knowing quite what to say, and then in a hushed tone she almost whispered, "*a panic attack.*"

"Alex can't understand it. He felt like he was dying, and even the ambulance officers thought it was his heart."

Rose, who had spent five years as a registered nurse before she had Christine's older sister Samantha, said, "It's not that uncommon Mary. It can feel that way; it's quite terrifying if you don't know what is happening. Well, good news anyway. Thank God it's not his heart," she said as Jessica rounded the corner.

"Whose heart?" Jessica chimed in.

"Got to go Mary," Rose said as she quickly hung up the phone.

Nanna Rose turned to Jessica.

"Whose heart?" Jessica repeated, now looking worried.

"Everything is fine, Jess," Nanna said as she moved in to give her a reassuring hug. Pulling away she placed her hands on Jessica's shoulders.

"Okay—dad was feeling unwell this morning, and he had to go to the hospital to see what was happening.

He's fine, all the results are normal. He can tell you all about it when he gets home," she said in a voice that conveyed she wasn't at all worried, when in fact she *was* worried. She had a nagging feeling in her own chest that told her that this may very well be just the beginning for Alex.

* * *

Alex sat in the waiting room of Gabriela Feliz, the psychologist who apparently was an expert in P.T.S.D., according to the cardiologist from St Vincent's Hospital. He felt like a fool. A panic attack for God's sake. *What...was he a five year old who was afraid to fly?* There was a part of him that just wanted to get up and leave, but he stayed seated. He needed answers, and he couldn't leave until he had them.

As he waited he reflected on the phone conversation that he had with his boss. Telling Huckett was hard. He didn't know quite what to say. He almost wished it had been a heart attack, at least he wouldn't be misjudged for that.

He heard the tone of his boss's voice change from accepting to something else less compassionate when he told him. Alex knew Huckett could never understand. To him, it would be a sign of weakness. To be honest, Alex was not so sure it wasn't, but the fact remained that he had absolutely no explanation for how, or why it had happened, or even what it was that he experienced on that day, and so reluctantly, here he was.

Gabriela Feliz walked into the waiting room and called his name.

"Alex Fredrick? Come through please."

Her consulting room was minimally decorated. There was an analogue clock placed surreptitiously in one corner on an occasional table, a floor lamp in the other corner and a selection of chairs and a sofa, all placed strategically about the room. Alex was directed to sit where ever he felt most at ease. He chose the comfortable arm chair facing the large landscape picture adorning the opposite wall. Gabriela Feliz sat adjacent to him, clipboard in hand and began to speak. She asked about the circumstances of Mark's death and how it was that Alex was told. She questioned him about all the details of that morning from when he found out, to when he reached the hospital, and what had happened then. She wanted to know if Alex had ever had anxiety or feelings of panic before. He shook his head no. She then went on to describe what she felt had happened.

It appears that when someone experiences a major trauma, such as the tragic death of your son—whether it is witnessed or not, the trauma can be so acute that, in an attempt to protect itself, the deeper mind may link the horrific event to certain things that were connected in some way to the trauma. When those triggers are experienced again, the body goes into panic mode because the deeper mind believes the danger is still happening. Unfortunately for Alex, he had two flights the day of Mark's death; one before he knew what had happened to his son and one directly after.

Gabriela went on to suggest that, because Alex's body was shocked by the devastating news he received that day, his conscious mind shut down and his subconscious mind—which is neither logical or literal — somehow connected the trauma with flying. Thus, when Alex subsequently began his journey to the airport, he began to feel more and more uneasy the closer he got to the actual plane, until he eventually had a full-on panic attack. Without therapy, she suggested that it would undoubtedly happen again.

"These things have a habit of getting worse each time the trigger is activated, due to the fact that the mind is learning the faulty response and getting better at it. Very soon Alex, you would be able to set it off just by thinking about it," she said.

"Not a very comforting thought," Alex replied, disheartened. "What can I do about it?"

"I'm glad you asked." she smiled.

"I would like to work with you to learn some effective cognitive strategies, to help recognise and challenge negative or faulty thoughts. However, because this is happening more on the subconscious level, I think we really need to go deeper. Have you ever heard of hypnotherapy?"

"Of course, but isn't that just stage show stuff?"

"No—on the contrary, 'stage show stuff' is hypnosis. Hypno*therapy* is a really effective therapeutic tool to get to the core of many issues that are not always apparent in the conscious mind."

"Did you know that our conscious mind is responsible for only around 7% of what we do? 93% of all functioning occurs at the subconscious level, and that's where hypnotherapy comes into its own. Would you be willing to give it a try?"

"Yes of course, if you think it will help."

"I do. Let's book you another appointment for two weeks' time and we can get to work on it."

Alex couldn't wait for two weeks, he needed to get to Sydney. He had offered Huckett a Skype meeting, but Huckett, had declined.

"No son, you take all the time you need to recover. Stay in the Melbourne office, keep the home fires burning. The meeting can wait, it's not that important. All in good time, Alex."

Huckett's words had been somewhat disturbing. *'It's not that important.'* What exactly had he meant by that? Alex knew that the future of the company *was* the most important thing for Stewart Huckett.

Was he changing his mind?

Did he now think Alex was not up for the job? Jesus—what if Huckett thought he was not up for the job? Shit! What the hell had happened to him at the airport anyway? Was he going crazy? Why had he lost total control of his body? Bloody hell, what next?

Alex was aware that Stewart Huckett was not a man of great patience. Generally, when he wanted something, he wanted it to happen yesterday. *'All in good time,'* was not a principle that could usually be applied when it came to Huckett. He was all business, all of the time. Alex wondered again if he had a hidden agenda, but then he quickly put those thoughts out of his mind. *Perhaps Huckett was just being compassionate after all.*

The words *'compassionate'* and *'Huckett'* generally did not go together, either. Alex knew this, and the seed of doubt was sewn.

Alex would not be beaten by this. He had flown literally hundreds of times and he never gave it a second thought. The airport was his second home for God's sake. He almost had a permanent seat in the business class lounge. He would go to Sydney tomorrow, just to show himself he could, but even as he thought these thoughts he felt a strange feeling in his stomach and chest forming; he ignored it.

He picked up the phone and dialled the airline service desk. He knew most of the attendants personally, and they always made his bookings quickly and efficiently.

'Hi Lorraine," he said as a friendly voice answered the call.

"Alex?, Is that you?"

"Yes, it's me."

"Are you all right? I heard they took you to hospital in an ambulance?"

As Alex thought of the incident at the airport his chest tightened and he became aware his heart was beginning to race.

"Yes, I'm fine, Lorraine. I can't explain it, but I got the all-clear. Good as gold now. Can you book me on the 7:15 to Sydney tomorrow morning?"

"Sure, will do. I'll send the booking details to your email. Gosh I'm glad you are okay; we were all worried."

"Thanks Lorraine," he said as he hung up the phone.

Lorraine thought she heard an unfamiliar tone in Alex Fredrick's voice. She was unsure what it was, but there was definitely something different about him today. She quickly attended to the booking, linked it to his email and pressed send. She started at 6am tomorrow. She would make a point of stopping by the business lounge to see how he was doing.

Alex was sitting on his bed when he dropped the phone and clutched his chest. He had broken out in a cold sweat. Terror had struck him. He could not breathe; it was happening again.

Hannah stood at the bedroom door of what was once her parent's bedroom. Her father had, over the last few days, taken to sleeping in the spare room. He said it was easier to sleep in there. She was puzzled to see him in his old room again. As he sat on the bed, her father looked distressed. He was pale and looked sweaty. He didn't see her silently looking in, and he didn't see her silently turn away and go back into her own room. She knew that he had been unwell and had been to hospital. She knew that an ambulance had taken him there, just like the ambulance that took her brother away. She shut her bedroom door quietly, picked up Pabby and hugged him tightly.

* * *

At the same time in another household just around the corner, Monica McKinley sat at her kitchen table, nursing a cup of lukewarm tea in both hands. She was lost in thought. Life in the McKinley family home had been different since the death of Mark Fredrick. She herself, was trying to make sense of this tragic loss. A loss to not only the Fredrick family, but to the community as a whole. It was staggering to notice just how many people had been impacted.

Monica was on the parent teacher association. She was the Year Twelve parent representative, and, as such, she had many of the Year Twelve parents come to her to talk about how their child was or was not coping with this tragedy. The significance and far reaching implications of a single event was hard to measure.

Together with the principal Greg Preston, the parents were very supportive of the programs and changes that had been implemented at the school, in an attempt to avoid this ever happening again at Green Valley Secondary College. To date, things were looking extremely positive. Programs had been smoothly integrated into the school co-curricular syllabus. There was now far more support for children who were struggling, but she worried about those who had already experienced the trauma of the death of their school captain, and a young girl with so much to look forward to. It was a double calamity that affected the whole school; the children, their friends, families and indeed the whole community, but, today, this was not Monica McKinley's major concern.

Monica knew, as she sat at the table lost in thought, that so many had been affected, but none more than her own son; she was worried. She had watched a gradual decline as her son Hamish struggled with his own demons, and she feared what he might do if he could not get the psychological support he needed. He had been to counselling to discuss the circumstances around Mark's death, but the fact remained: Hamish McKinley could not forgive himself for turning his back on his best friend.

Hamish was aware, logically, that Mark's death was not his fault, but there was a deeper part of him that told him something else. He had been fighting an ever-increasing sense of guilt every day. The counsellor had taught Hamish how to challenge these 'irrational' thoughts, and as much as he tried, there was another voice in his head that told him 'That's bullshit.' *After all what kind of a friend was he to just walk away when things got tough? He truly believed Mark would be alive today if he had been there to support and help him through whatever it was he was going through.*

Monica was now becoming increasingly worried for her son. She didn't know how to help him. They had always been so close; he had always told her everything that was bothering him, but she did not know how to reach him on this issue. She just didn't know how to get through the impenetrable facade he had put up. He had made up his mind that he was partially to blame and this belief was now slowly taking its toll. Hamish was not sleeping and insomnia was becoming a real issue that was affecting her son in many insidious ways. His marks had suffered greatly, which was no surprise to Monica as he barely put any effort into his studies these days. In fact, she worried that if he continued in this direction he may well fail his final year; but at the moment this was the least of her concerns. He looked tired because he *was* tired, and this weariness was causing him to be snappy, dismissive and distant. This was so out of character for her son, who now seemed to be permanently wearing a tangible sadness, a camouflage that hid the real Hamish from view; a deep and intensifying sadness that was beginning to envelope his whole persona.

Monika knew she had to do something, but what?

14

TAKE MY HAND

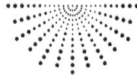

A lex did not make the flight, again.

That morning now seemed so long ago as he sat once again in the waiting room of Gabriela Feliz. He had cancelled the previous appointment with her, preferring to remain in a state of denial. He was fine. There must be another medical explanation he had thought, and he was going to find it, come hell or high water.

As he waited for his appointment, Alex reflected on the past weeks. He had gone to three doctors, and had several investigations and tests that all confirmed, medically he was well. Finally, a visiting resident doctor from Russia sat Alex down and spoke candidly to him.

"Alex, what is it that you do not want to accept about your psychological diagnosis?" He asked.

"I really don't know," said Alex.

"I live in the world of logic and reason. I'm always in control, and I like it that way. My family and my work have always depended upon it. I'm not crazy. I just don't know what is happening to me and there must be a logical answer. What the psychologist told me was not logical, far from it. This *'thing,'* it's happening more and more now, even when I'm nowhere near an aeroplane, which by the way, I have always loved. It just doesn't make any sense to me, and that's the scary part. I am a man of reason, a problem solver, I like being in control. My boss requires it, *I require it.*"

"Psychological issues don't have to make sense, Alex," Dr. Nikolai stated.

"I can tell you this: there is nothing medically wrong with you. From what you have told me, your diagnosis makes perfect sense. The body is amazing, Alex. Did you know that when you think any thought, your body powerfully responds automatically in an instant; physically, chemically and emotionally?

"Not really."

"It's true."

"A mere thought can cause a cascade of responses that can stop a grown man in his tracks. This is not a sign of weakness, Alex, it is a sign of the power and potential of your mind. The more you go looking for the symptoms that you really don't want, the more you will certainly find them, anytime, anywhere."

"I have come from a war zone, Alex. I was a medic in the second Chechen war, part of the airborne division. I have seen trauma, and nobody knows better than me, the effects that it can have on a human mind and body. The physical injuries were apparent, and *those* soldiers got help. The emotional issues were not so obvious. Many soldiers went home, if they were lucky, to struggle on their own. They weren't as fortunate as you, Alex. They had no diagnosis; they had no psychological services. Many like you were too proud to seek the help they required and because of this, many resorted to the same last option as your son." He paused so Alex could take in the bigger implications of his statement.

"I have suffered as you have." He continued. "I was one of the lucky ones who did get help. It's no shame to admit you need help, and you do need help, Alex. I would wholeheartedly advise you take it."

Alex sat in silence for a moment. He suddenly felt ashamed of himself. He hadn't even realised it, but he had inadvertently taken on the exact same mindset that causes people to feel embarrassment over having a mental illness.

The flood gates opened, and the truth suddenly flowed in. He could see it now. He would never have believed that he had a mental health prejudice, but there it was–he did. He had been embarrassed to tell anyone, ashamed to tell his boss. The irony and stupidity of this was now illuminated as though Dr. Nikolai had just turned on a light. How stupid he had been. Perhaps this was the reason Mark had chosen not to seek help. Perhaps he had learned to be ashamed of mental health struggles just like his father.

Alex stood, put out his hand to shake that of Dr. Nikolai.

"Thank you, doctor, I appreciate your candour. I think you just handed me a lifeline—things seem clearer now. I will take that help after all."

* * *

Gabriela Feliz appeared from around the corner of the waiting room.

"Alex, I can see you now," she smiled warmly.

They both entered the consulting room. This time he was more relaxed. He looked around with fresh eyes, noticing a comfortable black leather reclining chair in the far corner, slightly away from the other chairs. He wasn't sure if he had noticed that before.

Gabriela said, "Welcome back, Alex. I wasn't sure if I would see you again."

"I wasn't sure either," he said honestly.

"I am ready now though. My situation has worsened somewhat."

"Really? Well, that's not a problem, because we will get started today."

Alex went on to describe in detail the most recent incidents, such that now all he really had to do was hope like hell he wouldn't have a panic attack in the most inconvenient of places. The thought alone that it might happen was often enough to bring it on. It was definitely getting worse. He hadn't been to Sydney for his important meeting, which according to Stewart Huckett was not so important after all. In fact, he hadn't been to work at all for the last ten days. He was worried that if he went into the office he would have a panic attack in front of the junior partners, or worse, a client. He was feeling better about his diagnosis but, nonetheless, Alex Fredrick was the quintessential professional, and he would never allow that to happen. It was better for now that he worked from home and that is exactly what he did.

Gabriela nodded and took a lot of notes. She allowed Alex to talk about his concerns, all of which were noted down. She stated that although her therapy was solution focused, sometimes in order to know where they were heading, they both needed to look back briefly at where he had been. She then used this information to help Alex identify what he would feel like when this problem no longer existed.

"That's easy," said Alex, "I'll be normal again."

She pressed him for more detail. She really wanted to know what 'normal' was for Alex Fredrick; what it looked like and what it felt like. By the end of the discussion Alex had created an image that fully represented how he would be when this issue was no longer a problem. Words such as 'relief,' 'comfortable,' and 'confident,' were all a part of this image.

Gabriela went on to explain to Alex what hypnosis was, and more importantly, what hypnosis wasn't. She said that it was imperative for optimal results that Alex understood exactly what the process was. She would not be waving a magic wand. Hypnosis was nothing like what Alex had thought.

A hypnotic trance is an induced voluntary state, often combined with relaxation, that encouraged the client to focus on a fixed idea or concept, to the exclusion of everyday thoughts. Trance, she said, was a perfectly natural state. It's a little like being so engrossed in a movie that you don't really hear someone walk into the room, or being so focused on the computer or a book that you lose all sense of time and place.

She told Alex that the deeper mind cannot tell the difference between what we imagine to be true, and what is actually true.

"We can use this in hypnosis to our advantage. The conscious mind may be well aware that you are in the room in this chair, but your sub-conscious mind can take you anywhere. I want you to under-stand the process but I also need you to know what you have to do. The more vividly you can be wherever I take you, the better. If I suggest for you to bring to mind a happy memory, or a confident time from the past, I really need you to imagine it as though you are actu-ally there, almost as though it is happening right now. In doing so you can discover that it is possible to connect to that same feeling again, just by thinking about it vividly, almost like in a daydream. Your body will respond to your thoughts. Do you think you can do that for me, Alex?"

"Sure, I'll do my best."

"Great, so please remember, I will not be *doing* hypnosis *to you*, I'll be doing it *with you*. Okay?"

"As long as I don't walk like a chicken when I leave," he said with a wry smile.

"You know, I think I'm going to get a sign for my door that says: *No, you won't walk like a chicken.*" She rolled her eyes.

"Heard it before, I suppose?" said Alex.

"A few times. Okay, ready to make a start?"

"Yep."

"This will take as long as it takes, Alex. I want to start by just getting you used to the process. We'll begin by exploring the concept of change and how it's not only possible, it's inevitable. Okay?

"Okay."

"Right, are you ready to go into trance now? If so, please take a seat in the recliner."

Alex sat. There was something about this chair that made him feel relaxed already. He closed his eyes and followed Gabriela's straight-forward instructions.

Forty minutes passed as though it were only ten as he heard the sound of Gabriela's voice asking him to come back up to full conscious awareness.

"Wow," Alex said. "That was certainly different. I really didn't want to come back," he smiled a blissfully contented smile.

"How do you feel?" She asked.

"I feel so relaxed, more relaxed than I've felt in a very long time." He paused. "That was powerful. This may sound strange, but I now have a real sense of hope...not just about the panic attacks...*He turned his head to look directly at her*...but about Mark. I feel hopeful now."

Gabriela smiled. She looked truly moved.

Alex observed this woman in front of him. He was touched by her sincerity. He considered carefully what he would say next. This was work for her, but there was a strength about her that implied she could carry the weight of anything he had to declare, and he *did* have something to declare. He paused for a moment before he cautiously continued.

"You know the really strange thing was, I got a sense of Mark's presence in the room." He again paused to assess her response, before continuing. She simply smiled and nodded for him to go on. "For the first time, thinking about him didn't feel sad or painful. It felt almost peaceful. I know it sounds ridiculous, but it felt like he was here in the room with me."

He stopped again, as if to gauge her reaction to his words. She just nodded acceptingly.

He noted her acceptance, as he threw caution to the wind and said what he never believed he would ever say. "I felt him. He touched my hand and told me not to worry about him, that he was fine, he was at peace."

Alex was clearly moved by his experience and looked visibly emotional.

"It felt so real. I know it's crazy, but I believe he's okay now."

"That's wonderful," she said smiling.

"The subconscious mind is very powerful and not at all logical. Sometimes it brings forth the things that are most important for you to come to terms with at the time. It's really no surprise, I think we both recognise the significance. I am very careful to never lead or mislead you in these sessions. I would never suggest to you in trance what I believe, because I may be wrong. I can say, however, with complete honesty, that I have been doing this for long enough, that I have seen the most amazing things. We are all connected to a greater source; a universal energy that connects us all. If you say he was here with you, I believe he was. I have seen it before. Within you right now, is the most amazing ability to connect and to create. We all have untapped potential that we are yet to discover. Scientifically we are only scratching the surface of what is possible. You may very well have just experienced that potential and connected to your son on an energetic level. You have your own answers, Alex. Your mind knows the reasons that things are as they are. Your mind can create its own solutions. What I can say, with a fair amount of certainty, is that this issue is directly connected to Mark. This just reinforces that for me. I'm so pleased for you Alex" she said placing her hand over her heart, and she really was.

* * *

Mark observed what was occurring in the therapy room of Gabriela Feliz. He had noticed whenever he was close to his family, he could feel their grief and pain permeating through his energy field. They were all connected on this level and he was beginning to understand that they always would be.

It seemed to Mark that he was here for a reason. He looked for Grace, and she appeared beside him.

"I'm with you," she conveyed without words.

"You will know your purpose."

Mark returned his attention to his father. It disturbed him to know that his whole family was all suffering so much.

He watched on as the therapist guided his father into a deep state of relaxed, yet focused, awareness, which allowed Alex to connect directly with his subconscious mind, leaving his analytical conscious mind far behind.

Mark desperately wanted to communicate with his father in some way, to let him know that he was all right.

"What can I do?" he pleaded, looking for guidance from his wise companion.

"Trust," Grace said.

Mark felt overwhelming love begin to intensify within his presence as he looked upon his father. He moved in closer and allowed that beautiful energetic field to engulf them both. As it did, he felt a sacred connection begin to strengthen. A connection he instantly recognised had transcended many lifetimes.

His bodiless form reached out and touched his father's hand, their energies entwined and the synergy of this strengthened the healing love that could be felt by them both.

"I'm here," Mark whispered in a voice that could only be heard by his father.

"I'm fine. Please do not worry about me. I am at peace now."

"I'm so sorry, dad."

"I love you."

He stayed in his father's presence, enjoying the sacred connection they were sharing, knowing that, as he did, it was in some way helping his father to heal.

"We will be together again," were the last words he said as he allowed his father's energetic field to once again separate from his own.

* * *

Alex left the rooms of Gabriela Feliz after making a follow-up appointment for two weeks' time. He felt somehow uplifted and peaceful yet also very emotional about what he had just experienced. He considered what he would do next. He had an important meeting this afternoon scheduled at the firm; it was one meeting he could not handle from home. Because he was the senior partner in charge, it was expected that he would be present at all such meetings, but not today. He considered what he would say. He knew it would get back to Huckett, but today, he didn't care.

He called the office to say he would not be coming in that afternoon. He told Roselyn, who manned reception, that Roger was fully briefed and he would be able to handle everything. He instructed her to schedule a nine o'clock meeting the following day, for him to be appraised of the proceedings. He then hung up the phone. He gave no explanation. He would deal with explanations tomorrow. Today, he just needed to reflect on his experience.

Alex Fredrick was a man who did not wear his emotions on his sleeve, yet today there was a part of him that felt as if he just wanted to cry, and not stop until he had released all the pent-up pain and emotion that he had stored in his body over the last five months. He could not work today. He was too distracted, too emotional. He had never expected this. He would have dismissed it as lunacy if anyone else had told him such nonsense, but he *did not* want to dismiss this. He didn't want to just continue on with his day as though nothing had happened. He needed time to digest all that *had* happened. He wanted to remember and hold on to that wonderful feeling.

Alex returned home. Christine was sitting in the living room, still in her dressing gown looking distant and cold. It was as though she was here in body only. Her mind was far, far away. He knew not where. He was not able to connect with her anymore, and he had long since given up trying.

He longed for the Christine of old. He wanted to tell her of his experience, but he did not know where to begin. Would she believe him, or would she dismiss it as insanity? Right now, he wasn't about to take that chance. He did not want this experience to be tainted by negativity, not today. He just wanted to hold onto this feeling for as long as possible, a feeling that connected him in some way to his son.

Alex went upstairs. He was heading for his room. He had been sleeping in the spare room for some time now. It was a choice he had made for self-preservation. Seeing his beautiful wife lost in her own prison of agonising despair, as she was unable to reach her hand out for help, was something he could no longer watch. It was destroying him; he had to distance himself from it. They were now like strangers living under the same roof. It was a situation he would never have believed was possible.

"Christine and Alex Fredrick, the perfect forever couple." Not anymore.

As Alex walked up the stairs he passed his daughter's room.

Jessica was at school, but Hannah was in her bedroom.

Hannah was sitting on her bed colouring in. His troubled daughter had come no closer to speaking. She was still so very withdrawn from the world.

Benny lay curled up on the soft beige carpet. Even he had been affected by the tragedy of what had taken place under the Fredrick family's roof. He simply did not understand what had happened to his joyful, buoyant little companion. It had been some time since Benny had even been walked. Nanna Rose and Jessica were possibly the only ones to have walked Benny in the last few months, but neither could persuade Hannah to come along.

Alex made a note to himself that he would take Benny out this afternoon.

He bent down to pat his dog who was now glancing up at him through sad eyes, without lifting his head off the floor. He appeared lethargic; his usually over-energetic tail was motionless.

Alex looked at his daughter who was now aware of his presence, but, ignoring him, continued colouring in.

"Hi sweetheart," he said.

How's Benny going?" "You know I think we should take him out for a walk this afternoon. It's a beautiful day. I think he would like that. He's been looking a bit sad lately. Do you think he is sad?"

"Yes, you know I think he probably is," Alex sat on the bed, continuing his heartfelt monologue to his silent daughter.

"I think he is missing Mark too, but you know what, Hannah? I think he feels sad because you are sad. He really does love you, doesn't he?

There's really no denying, he *is* your dog." Alex prayed that in some small way he was getting through to his daughter.

He had her attention and although she continued to colour, he felt she was listening. He hesitated, unsure if he should go ahead or not, but he needed to speak. Why would he have been given this spiritual experience, if not to help himself and those around him.

He continued on, "Hannah, I want to tell you something I think will make you feel better."

Alex felt so safe to speak of his experience to Hannah of all people. After all, who better than a child who would never judge him? A child who, on some level, was still innocent enough to believe in fantasy and possibilities? Or had this experience stripped her of all her childhood innocence? He hoped not.

"Hannah, today I had the most extraordinary experience."

She stopped colouring, but did not look at him.

"Today I went to a lady who wanted to help me with my feelings about Mark."

Hannah selected a black pencil and began harshly and deliberately scribbling over a part of her drawing.

Alex ignored her scribbling and continued on. "She helped me get very relaxed, Hannah. I had to sit in a big black leather chair that reclined and close my eyes, and Hannah," he looked directly at his daughter, "When I got *very* relaxed I had the most comforting experience."

Hannah stopped again; pencil poised just above the page.

"I really don't know if it was real or not, but it felt so real."

"Other than the lady, I haven't told anyone else. It seems so crazy Hannah, but I really think Mark came to me today."

Hannah put the black pencil down and did not look at her father.

"He was talking to me, Hannah."

Alex wondered how much to say to this damaged little person. How much could she take? He hoped that it may help her in some way to hear this, and it certainly helped him to talk about it.

He continued on with the greatest caution.

"He told me he was all right."

"He said not to worry about him, that he was in a beautiful place." He paused before continuing.

"He touched my *hand,* Hannah," Alex almost whispered, and as he did the emotion of that memory began to bubble up from deep inside of him again as tears began to form in his eyes.

"Right here," he pointed to the back of his right hand.

Alex's hand was resting on the pink doona that was adorning Hannah's bed. For an entire minute there was silence, neither moved, and then Hannah reached over and placed her little hand over Alex's, covering the exact spot that he had just pointed to.

They sat there like that for a few moments, together in their own thoughts before the silence was broken by the most beautiful words Alex had ever heard.

"He comes here."

Alex stared at his daughter; *did she just speak?* He wasn't sure.

Had he just heard that, or was he imagining it?

She still did not look at him.

He placed his other hand on top of hers and they sat without speaking. The tears that had been welling in his eyes were now spilling down his cheeks.

Hannah looked up at him and for the first time since Mark's death she made eye contact with him and she spoke. This time there was no questioning what he heard.

"He comes to me at night. He talks to me."

Alex stared at his daughter. The feelings within him were confusing and confronting—but mostly they were comforting. There was hope, there was real hope. It was going to take a while to process all of this, but for now, hope was enough.

Alex leaned over and hugged Hannah. He held her tightly, and in that moment he felt his heart expanding with the purest love that seemed to radiate out of his own chest toward his youngest daughter, engulfing them both.

"Oh Hannah, there are so many things I do not understand," he said as he turned to face her. "I believe he came to me today too, and that makes me very happy."

He wondered if he would be able to talk to Christine about all of this, now that there was so much more to tell, but he would have to give that some more thought. Today he just wanted to hold onto this feeling.

"I'm going to take Benny for a walk," he concluded, deliberately not offering an invitation to his daughter.

"Come on Benny, let's get your lead."

Benny lifted his head and slowly got to his feet. His tail gave one wag and he followed Alex out of the room.

They stepped outside as the front door closed behind them. It was a beautiful winter's day. The chill in the air was overridden by the feeling created from the rich blue of the sky, dotted with patches of fluffy white clouds. Together, these things contributed to the sense of optimism that came with the promise of impending spring.

Hannah waited quietly under the branches of the liquid amber that was the centrepiece of the Fredrick's front garden. Its naked branches were beginning to display the tiny buddings that were an assurance of the green foliage to come. She was dressed in her coat for the winter cool outside as she waited patiently for her father and Benny to appear.

As Alex walked down the path, he did not immediately notice his younger daughter, but Benny certainly did. He pulled sharply on his lead, freeing himself from Alex's grasp as he bounded excitedly toward her. She knelt down and hugged her dog.

"Benny," she whispered.

Benny's tail wagged so fast that it threatened to lift him right off the ground. This made Hannah giggle ever so slightly. As Alex watched on, the sight of his daughter reconnecting to life after such a long time warmed his heart.

Today was a good day.

He felt that, in many ways, he had turned a corner. There was so far to go, but this was a start.

"Wonderful to see you are joining us, Hannah," Alex said.

"Perhaps we could ask Mark to walk with us too."

Hannah reached up and took her father's hand. He did not have words to describe the comfort that came from his daughter's unexpected gentle touch. It was blissful. A happiness, combined with the bittersweet reality that he would never again hold the hand of his son in such a way, overcame him. However, as they walked with Benny leading the way, he imagined in that moment that Mark *was* hand in hand with them, walking alongside them both. He could almost feel his presence.

He smiled, not knowing that Mark *was* right by his side, smiling too.

15

DROWNING, NOT WAVING

Christine had sunk just about as low as she could go. Everyone could see it, not least of all herself. There were only one of two ways to go from here. She could choose to make the same choice as her troubled son had made, or she could begin the painful journey of reconnecting to life. Despite the fact that she had reached the point where she really did not want to live anymore without her precious son, there were two reasons that stopped her from taking the option that offered an end to her pain. Those two reasons were her girls.

Even at her lowest of lows, she would never ever be able to do that to them. They had been hurt enough. To hurt them any more was unthinkable, and this very fact was the fragile lifeline that kept Christine connected to the real world and managed to keep her head just above water. For Christine, the ripples from her son's death were now becoming a tsunami of grief that was threatening to drown her, and would have already taken her under if not for Hannah and Jessica.

It was now five months since the death of Mark. But for Christine it still felt like yesterday. She half expected to see him coming through the front door after school, dropping his bag in the middle of the hallway as he ran to the kitchen to raid the cupboards for a snack before training. Weekends were particularly difficult. They had always been so filled with sporting competitions and training, and the void left a cavernous hole so wide in the fabric of their weekends that she had now lost herself in the depths of it. The girls did not participate in sport in the same way that Mark had. Mark had indeed been a hard act to follow.

Jessica had always been more interested in music and drama, participating in the school pantomimes and theatrical productions, while Hannah just loved to dance. She had done tap and jazz since she was six, but most of all she loved free dance. It allowed her to express herself unreservedly through simple un-choreographed movements. Improvised freestyle dance was the perfect fit for the spontaneous free spirit of Hannah; but life had taken its toll, and Christine wondered if she would ever see her free-spirited daughter dance again.

Jess looked forward to the school production the most. This year, the school was putting on *Mary Poppins*. The lead roles were sought-after, and due to the amount of preparation required for these events, auditions were held in the first two weeks of the school year. Jess had secured the role of Mrs. Winifred Banks. She was ecstatic at the time. The role had several singing parts and was quite the coup for a Year Nine girl, as these major roles generally went to Year Eleven and Twelve students. Jessica could not contain her joy when she was awarded the coveted role, and the family had a celebratory dinner to acknowledge her exciting accomplishment.

Christine reflected on these happier memories as she silently recognised the fact that the Green Valley Secondary College's gala performance of *Mary Poppins* was due to be staged in the main auditorium in two weeks' time. The role of Mrs. Winifred Banks would now be played by Year Eleven student, Francine Tolegate. Jessica had retreated from everyday life in so many ways since Mark's death, forgoing so many things that she had once enjoyed. The school production was one of them.

Christine had resigned herself to the fact that her marriage was now but a shell of what it used to be, and, for the life of her she just couldn't do anything about that. As much as Alex had initially tried to fix what was so badly broken, she was sure he had now given up.

She blamed herself for this too. She had allowed it all to happen and now it seemed there was no going back. Alex had long since moved into the spare bedroom and was spending more and more time at work.

He had told her about his second visit with the therapist. He had seemed so reassured by it, so ready to believe, but Christine had mercilessly shot it all down in flames as the fanciful projections of a pained mind. It was as though she just couldn't allow him to feel peace. Mark was dead, and that was that. He had not visited Alex, for God's sake! He was dead! This story was nothing more than the delusions of a grieving father, and his attempts to make himself feel better. Who was this therapist anyway, and why was she preying on the vulnerable in such an unforgivable way? Christine had been so vitriolic and so hurtful about the whole episode that Alex never mentioned it again.

Day by day, Alex helped Hannah find her way back from the distant place she had been inhabiting for all this time. Very slowly, as words returned to her, his daughter was reappearing. Not the carefree innocent Hannah of the past, because he feared her innocence was now lost forever, but a new Hannah. Somehow different for what she had been through, yet somehow the same.

They sat together each night and Alex would read to her. They would then talk about Mark. It was within this talking that they both began the healing process. They remembered the funny times and they sometimes found themselves so lost in the memories that they would laugh together at some little detail; a *"remember when"* moment. It felt good to laugh. It felt somehow healing, as a dark and heavy weight was being lifted off their souls.

Hannah said Mark still visited her, but not as much now. They talked about these times, and for Hannah it was so natural; it was something she just accepted. For Alex it felt comforting and reassuring; a connection to his son through space and time. It didn't make sense to his analytical mind, but there was no denying his own extraordinary experience. He couldn't talk to anyone else about this in the house. Christine would not listen, and Jessica would never believe him, or perhaps she would, he mused, so for now it was something that remained a special bond between father and daughter. Something that was helping them both to move forward. A spiritual encounter they had both shared in their own way, that inextricably linked them and supported them as they attempted to navigate the next steps in their individual lives without Mark.

* * *

As the days passed the ever-present wedge that had been driven between Alex and Christine continued to widen, until the day in early spring when Christine sank to her lowest ebb. After Mark's death, Christine had thought life could not get any worse, but she was wrong. She had since, unknowingly but systematically, been on a path of destruction, affecting everything and everybody around her.

Hannah had now returned to school, and, for the most part, things were going well, except for one particular Friday afternoon in late September. It was art class, and Hannah had been quietly standing at her easel with her art smock on to protect her clothes from the paint and indelible inks they had been using, as she focused her attention to the task at hand. They were experimenting with different types of drawing materials and multiple application methods. The task they were challenged with today was to draw fruit. There were various pieces of fruit strategically placed on the main table in the middle of the room, and the children positioned themselves around this and began creating their artwork. They were to use multiple types of applicators and different materials, to explore the various effects they could achieve. Hannah had selected the bright orange acrylic paint and a sponge applicator, to paint a life-sized orange, right up in the left-hand corner of the large art sheet. She stood back and observed. She was quite happy with the outcome. The sponge had adequately been able to produce something that looked a very similar consistency to orange skin. Miss Langhorne came over and praised Hannah for her life-like orange.

"That's great, Hannah. Now perhaps try some of the other application methods and some other materials. You have plenty of paper left there." She smiled inwardly, acknowledging her liking for this little girl, and her admiration for all she had overcome. She wanted Hannah to get more involved in art and all the other classes, as she used to, and it was finally beginning to happen.

Hannah smiled. She surveyed the table of fruit for what she might draw next. She spotted a large bunch of purple grapes. They looked like a bunch of little purple balloons. Hannah put down the orange paint-soaked sponge and carefully selected a thick brush and loaded it with purple indelible ink. She stood in front of her easel, paint brush poised to find the exact position to place her grapes when Alysha Mulligan, with her long blonde pony tails tied up in red ribbon bows, walked up to her. Alysha, who should have been at her own easel, looked at Hannah's orange.

"Not bad," she said examining the piece with her arms crossed. "Mine's better though"

Hannah just looked at her without speaking.

Then, Alysha, who was obviously spoiling for trouble went on to say, "Your brother has gone to Hell. My Mum said so." She stopped and waited for Hannah to react. Hannah looked shocked and confused. Why would this girl say such a horrid thing?

"Jesus said he was a sinner, and sinners go to Hell," Alysha continued in a righteous tone.

Hannah frowned, and then her frown contorted into an angry scowl. She glanced at the paintbrush in her hand laden with dark purple indelible ink. A second passed, she didn't think, she just acted. Seconds later Alysha's face and fine blonde hair were stained the deepest shade of purple. Hannah brushed two decisive strokes over her cheek through her hair, the resulting vibrant purple cross appeared as Hannah shouted two words with deep indignation: "YOU'RE WRONG!"

Alysha screamed for the teacher who immediately looked horrified.

"What's going on?" she demanded.

"Nothing! I didn't do anything." Alysha sobbed as she looked at her own hair. "She just painted me. It's in my hair, it's in *MY HAIR!*" The distress in her voice was audible and growing by the second.

"I want my mum, *NOW!*" She screamed.

"Oh, Hannah!" said Miss Langhorne as she turned her gaze toward her with a look of concern. "What have you done?"

Hannah did not say a word.

Alysha Mulligan was taken by the hand out of the room by Miss Langhorne into the teacher's bathroom to run water on her hair and face, but the damage was done. The marks would not easily be removed. Fortunately, this was only a semi-permanent ink, but nonetheless, Alysha would be wearing this cross on her cheek for days to come.

Alysha's mother was called. She arrived at the school to collect her distressed daughter and loudly declared to all within earshot, "What kind of child does such a thing, what a horrendous little horror!"

"There is obviously something very wrong in that household when one child commits the ultimate sin against God, and another child is uncontrollably violent to an innocent little girl."

Miss Langhorne was shocked to hear these words flowing so easily from Mrs. Mulligan's mouth, but she did not finish there.

She turned to her daughter and asked, "How did this happen darling?"

"I don't know," she sobbed. "I just said her orange was good."

"See, she was just being nice, complimenting the little horror. It's obvious that child cannot be around civilised children. This is completely unacceptable. I want her removed from the school permanently," she demanded.

"Schedule me an appointment with the principal," she ordered Jane Langhorne. "Make it soon—and while I'm at it, you should be reprimanded too. *You* let this happen," she said, pointing a finger aggressively toward the teacher.

"If you had been properly supervising the children, this would never have happened in the first place."

"I'm taking Alysha home right now, and she will stay home until this terrible purple violation has vanished," she said as she pointed aggressively to her daughter's stained face.

"I won't have my daughter ridiculed or bullied by the other children!" she exclaimed in a fit of rage as her own face turned a slight shade of purple.

Jane Langhorne could see one prominent pulsating vein protruding from her forehead.

"Please calm down, Mrs Mulligan."

"Don't tell me to calm down!" she said in a seething voice as she grabbed Alysha's hand with a little too much force and stormed out of the room, dragging her child behind her.

As it happened, the principal was at an in-service day when the incident occurred, but as 'Hurricane Mulligan' left the building, Jane

Langhorne braced herself and reluctantly picked up the phone to inform her principal of the unfortunate situation.

Christine had been called to pick up Hannah until the school could decide what should be done about the incident. She had started drinking early this particular day, to 'calm her nerves,' or so she claimed. The fact was it numbed her, for a while at least, but she was requiring more and more to achieve the same effect. When the school had called, she had been told there had been an *'incident'* with Hannah involving ink and another child. She was asked to arrange for Hannah to be picked up from outside the main office where she would be waiting.

Without thought Christine picked up her keys and bag and headed to the car. She reversed out of the driveway and made her way towards the school, aware that the alcohol in her system would probably put her close to, if not over, the blood alcohol state limit of 0.05, but she felt fine. The school was only a few streets away; she would be okay, she thought.

It was just after 2:30 and the 40km school zones were active. Christine did not notice that her speedometer was reading 70km as she rounded the corner heading toward the school car park. She also did not notice Peter Yorgason, a Grade Four boy who was leaving school early to attend a dentist appointment, step out onto the pedestrian crossing twenty metres in front of her, until it was almost too late. She slammed on the brakes skidding and sliding on the wet road until her car finally came to a halt in the middle of the crossing. Her car stopped just centimetres away from Peter who was frozen in his tracks, standing staring at the car that had nearly hit him. Their eyes met, both frozen in that moment, in absolute shock at what had nearly transpired. Both knew it, both felt the massive surge of adrenalin shoot through their respective bodies that told them absolutely, but for a split second, things could have been disastrously different. The lollipop lady who was still putting up the flags ran to the child and yelled abuse at Christine.

"What the hell were you thinking?"

Christine did not move for a good minute. She just stared ahead almost unable to move. Her hands were fixed, tightly gripping the steering wheel and her foot which was firmly planted on the brake, began to shake uncontrollably.

Oh my God, you nearly killed a child...you stupid, stupid, stupid, woman. Jesus Christ!

Christine went pale; she was in shock. She couldn't bring herself to get out of the car. Her legs would not allow her to stand up. She wound down her window with shaky hands.

"I'm so sorry, I'm so sorry, I'm so sorry, " was all she could say.

"You were speeding!" snapped the lollipop lady as she continued to comfort the young boy.

"I'm reporting you to the school."

"Okay," Christine said without objection, suddenly feeling very sober. The two pedestrians made their way to the safety of the footpath. A small crowd of early parents was gathering to see what was going on. They had heard the screech of brakes on the bitumen and the sound of raised voices. Christine felt ashamed. She drove her car through the crossing with the utmost caution, rounded the block and made her way back home and called her mother to collect Hannah.

Christine went into the kitchen and stood with her hands on the sink supporting herself. The image of the near collision flashed through her mind. She again saw the eyes of that young boy staring in horror as her vehicle stopped mere centimetres away from him.

The muscles of her jaw began to tremble as she finally succumbed to the enormity of her grief. Tears began to flow, hot and salty on her cheek like a tiny stinging stream flowing from the source of her pain, but then the stream became an unstoppable torrent. Her tears were heartbreaking and sincere, and she allowed herself to sob openly for the first time since the funeral. She held nothing back. A complete surrender to her grief allowed for the floodgates to open wide, and once opened, she had no resources, and more importantly no desire to stop it.

She cried not only for a young boy who today was spared disaster purely by the grace of God, but also for the pain she had held that had intensified almost daily for over six months now. Pain she had suppressed so deeply within her being that it had soured her relationship with all those that really cared about her.

This outpouring was desperately needed. Finally, unable to hold her own body weight, she slid down to the floor where she cried some more. She held nothing back, and it felt good to finally let go. She openly and loudly sobbed a heartfelt agonising howl that comes unashamedly from a mother who has lost her son. When she could cry no more, she remained on the floor, so utterly spent that for some time to come, she could not move.

Time passed; she was unsure of how long, before she finally felt she could stand. She slowly got to her feet and straightened her clothing. She glanced at her reflection in the kitchen window and for the first time in so long, she really saw herself. She looked puffy and blotchy from the tears that had flowed. It was as though the last six months had aged her ten years. She ran her fingers through her unruly hair and splashed some water on her face. She then walked past the wine rack toward the laundry and the secret cupboard where she kept her hidden stash, so nobody would know just how much she had been drinking. She opened the cupboard door and pulled out the remaining seven unopened bottles, which had been strategically placed behind several infrequently used items, so that they were obscured from view. She then proceeded to open every bottle of wine, those that had been hidden and those that had been on display in the wine rack, and poured them all down the sink.

She collected all the empty bottles and put them in the recycle bin that was just near the front gate. Tonight was bin night, tomorrow they would be gone forever. She took the bin out to the nature strip. The rattle of the bottles made her feel nauseated. She never wanted to hear that sound coming from her bin again.

Christine had had a massive shock, but shock had been what was needed for her to realise what she still had to lose. She felt so very grateful that she had not struck that young boy and caused another mother to have to go through the pain and grief that she herself was enduring. She knew that if she had hit that child while driving under the influence, she would never have been able to go on. She would most probably have gone to jail for manslaughter, dangerous driving and driving under the influence of alcohol. It had taken this for her to recognise just how low she had sunk. This was the point where she had to choose, and choose she did. In that moment as she sat frozen in her car, she had seen the truth flash before her eyes. She knew it was time. She was now aware she had hit rock bottom and if she were to stay in this life there was only one way to go from here. Now she would begin the long haul back.

Nanna Rose went to the school to collect Hannah from where she was sitting outside the principal's office. Hannah, who had been doing so well in her recovery, appeared to have retreated within herself once again. As Nanna Rose approached, she said in a gentle voice, "Hi Hannah, what's happened?"

Hannah just stared at the floor without saying a word.

Jane Langhorne had been paged to come out of class to explain what had gone on, but to be honest, she had no idea. She had asked Hannah what had happened, but Hannah had refused to speak. It seemed that none of the other children had seen what had led up to the painting disaster, and the scuffle that ensued. Actually, nobody seemed to see or hear anything at all, other than what happened after Alysha screamed, except for one child who was sure she heard Hannah say in an angry voice, "You're wrong!" Jane was inclined to believe what this child thought she'd heard because it might just explain the almighty purple 'X' that now adorned Alysha's right cheek.

Hannah had never been disruptive or disrespectful in class before. It was so out of character. Jane was aware that she had been through so much in the last six months, but aggressive behaviour was so foreign for Hannah. Even in her pain and distress she had never been aggressive, quite the opposite. She had retreated from the world, not struck out at it. This behaviour did not make sense. Something had certainly triggered it, of that, Jane Langhorne had no doubt. She would do her best to get to the bottom of it, but Alysha's parents wanted Hannah's head on a platter. Jane would need to proceed with caution. Currently, however, in the absence of any other explanation, she had no other option than to take Alysha's version of what happened to the principal tomorrow. She told Rose that an incident report would need to be written and Hannah would probably need to stay home from school until a disciplinary decision had been made.

That night in Hannah's bedroom, as Alex sat on her bed for their usual evening chat, he looked closely at his daughter. He had been told what had occurred at school that day, and he wanted to find out more. Hannah had not spoken to anyone about what had happened, but perhaps she would speak to him.

"Dad, what's a sinner?" she asked, before he had a chance to speak.

"Why do you ask?" Alex replied with curiosity.

Hannah shrugged.

"It's someone who has committed a sin, I suppose," said Alex.

"Is Mark a sinner?"

"No Hannah, Mark is not a sinner. Who told you that?"

"Alysha Mulligan."

"Really? Well she's wrong, Hannah."

"She said that Mark has gone to Hell, her mum said so."

"Well her mum is definitely wrong too, Hannah. Mark has not gone to Hell. We both saw him and he told us he was okay. Mrs Mulligan is definitely mistaken, " he reiterated to reassure her.

"Is that why you painted Alysha?"

"She said that Jesus said Mark is a sinner, and sinners go to Hell."

Alex leaned over and hugged his daughter. *Who would say such a thing to a little girl who has just lost her brother*, he thought to himself *and what kind of a mother would say that to her daughter?* Alex was disgusted.

"She's wrong isn't she?" Hannah whispered.

"I told her she was wrong. I didn't mean to paint her, it just happened."

"It's okay Hannah, I'll call Miss Langhorne tomorrow and we'll sort it all out."

He hugged his daughter again and he thought to himself that he *probably would have painted her too.*

The next morning, Alex contacted Hannah's teacher to inform her of what Alysha had said to Hannah. It was a very short phone call.

"Oh, she did, did she?" was Jane Langhorne's response.

"Thank you Alex, that is very helpful. I'm about to speak to the principal now. I'll let you know the outcome."

Personally, Jane Langhorne did not want to further discipline Hannah, but the school needed to be seen to be taking action. After all, they could not condone the behaviour, no matter how disgracefully provoked it had been. Hannah was given a two-week suspension, one week of which happened to fall in the school holidays.

Mrs. Mulligan was also spoken to with regard to her religious views.

She was instructed that both she and her daughter in future should refrain from sharing potentially hurtful opinions with other students who may be offended by them. Naturally, she was very unhappy with this outcome and threatened to report the school and the teachers involved to the State Education Department. Jane Langhorne courteously gave her the email address.

* * *

While the members of the Fredrick household were all in some way enduring and processing the painful aftermath and effects of the death of their beloved Mark, just around the corner, the McKinley family were continuing on with their own struggle.

Monica had settled into a new kind of normal. Her son was completing his V.C.E. final year without his best friend, and this alone was incomprehensible. Hamish had suffered silently, under the ever-watchful eye of his mother. He had borne his heavy burden of guilt for not being around when his best mate needed him the most. He had judged himself harshly for this, and it had affected him in ways that were obvious and ways that were unseen. He had distanced himself from people for a while, and it was almost as though he had lost trust in himself to be able to be a friend to anyone. There was a part of him that preferred it this way. It was somehow easier to not have to worry about anyone else, but there was one person who would not allow him to sit in his self-imposed isolation. That person was Catherine Belford.

After many months of trying to connect with her son on an emotional level, and always finding him to be just out of reach, a worried Monica McKinley resorted to seeking the help from one of Hamish's peers. She had seen how motivated Catherine had been about creating programs within the school, to help students navigate the difficult and often confusing world they found themselves in.

Catherine, with a wisdom far beyond her years, had with the

assistance of Greg Preston, implemented a group that met weekly in confidence to talk openly about anything that was concerning them. Students helping other students, and all the stigma about seeking help was released as the message was clear: 'everyone struggles sometimes.'

Catherine was insistent in her intention to get help for those who needed it the most. She met with the Principal and even went to the school council to discuss and ask for funding to bring a mindfulness meditation instructor into the school. This was a tangible and simple way to assist students, not only to bring calm into their lives, but also to allow them to gain clarity and build resilience. Catherine had tracked down a trusted and respected practitioner who was also passionate about adolescent mental health. She badgered the school council almost daily, until they had finally agreed to continuously run the mindfulness program at lunchtimes throughout the terms.

Catherine had personally practiced mindfulness and meditation for several years. She had grown up with it and had even attended mindfulness retreats with her mother. She was passionate about it and she brought this enthusiasm to the programs she had implemented.

When Monica approached her to see if there was any way she thought Catherine could assist Hamish to move on from his pain and the guilt he felt over the loss of his best friend, Catherine was more than eager to assist.

"Absolutely, " she said to Monica.

"This is exactly why I started this group. I'll talk to him and see if I can get him involved in some way."

Catherine approached Hamish to ask him to join her in participating in, and possibly helping to coordinate, the student groups, which had already been running for a few months. The groups, prompted by Greg Preston's initial call to action, had been established in the wake of Mark and Stacey's deaths, to assist others who were struggling.

Catherine convinced Hamish that there was nothing that could be done about what 'was,' but there was something that he could do to play a positive part in changing the future outcomes of other troubled students if he chose to join her.

For Hamish, this began to feel like a way that he could find some value in his experience. The silver lining, a purpose, the only thing that made sense to him in all the insanity. This was something positive to come out of all of the tragedy.

That was a month ago now, and was just what Hamish had needed. Catherine had invited him to participate in the mindfulness sessions, with a view to being able to recognise unhelpful thoughts and allow them to be released without judgement. Reflecting back now, Hamish knew that this had been pivotal for him and his own personal recovery. The ability to just be present in this moment, without the constant and continual rumination that he had been experiencing about things he should have done or could have said, was a godsend. The valuable lesson he had now learned, which was so simple yet so surprisingly difficult to initially grasp, was that there were certain things that were not within his control—to worry about these things was a fruitless endeavour. Hamish had experienced an overwhelming feeling of liberation when he discovered that the present moment is the only moment that we actually have.

He learnt how to use his breath to centre and ground himself, and what a difference it had made. Hamish could hardly believe just how quickly his body responded physically and emotionally when he began to take control of his thoughts; it was empowering. It gave him a tangible respite from his own previously damaging thoughts, and it allowed him to see all thoughts as just passing things. He learned that he was *not* his thoughts, that he was here before them and he would most definitely be here after them. Most importantly, he learned that he always got to choose which ones to focus on and which ones to just let pass him by.

Hamish found the principles of mindfulness so beneficial to his own healing that he began practising every day. The more he practised, the better he felt, and it was only now that he *was* feeling better, that he could look back and really appreciate just how far he had come on this journey, and how easily it could have had a very different outcome.

He learned quickly and attended nearly every session with Catherine, where to the best of his understanding, he would help the younger children grasp the concepts of mindfulness. It was good for the younger students to see that the Year Twelves needed help too, and that they were fully embracing these concepts. This created a feeling of inclusion and lack of judgement. It was beneficial for Hamish to know that in some way he was helping to prevent other students from encountering disaster.

Hamish smiled as he began to recognise the comforting realisation, that this was actually Mark's unintended gift. Inadvertently, Mark had been the catalyst that had created a safety net, in the form of school support groups, that would forever after catch other students who were struggling, before they fell into the darkness that had entrapped his friend.

16

AND SO IT GOES

Hamish McKinley was learning how to *live* with his painful thoughts, instead of fighting against them. He had managed to find a new perspective about all that had happened with his best friend, and, in doing so, he was able to discover a certain degree of peace. He desperately missed Mark and still struggled with understanding how Mark had reached the point of no return without his noticing, but now he had tools to help him deal with these thoughts.

Since discovering mindfulness, Hamish could now allow these thoughts to just be thoughts. Not something he needed to solve, because he was now discovering that some things could *not* be solved. Some things were unfair, some were painful and some had no available answer. He was now learning how to feel all right with that. He was quite astounded just how quickly things had turned around for him. Catherine had been his saving grace. She had not allowed him to disappear further from life. She had put out her hand and he had taken it, as she shone a light in the darkness for him to follow and find his way back, and this he did.

Everything had improved. He was now sleeping through the night, and, when he did wake, he had the tools to quickly and effectively go back to sleep. He was beginning to understand that the one thing that had been threatening to destroy him, making him feel so terribly bad and keeping him awake at night, was his own thoughts. When he learnt how to keep these under control, the world changed for him in so many ways. Sleep had been an essential coping factor that was missing from his life, and this had compounded everything else. Without sleep, there was no recovery.

Hamish had learned some very valuable lessons during this terrible time that would stay with him throughout his life, and for that he was grateful. He had found the only positive that had come out of all the devastation. This was comforting for him because it meant that Mark had not died in vain.

Monica McKinley looked on from a distance. Her protective maternal gaze was ever-watchful for signs of her son's concerning behaviours, but instead she began to notice that Hamish was reconnecting with life. There had been a noticeable change in him since she had first spoken to Catherine now over a month ago. He looked more at peace. He said he was sleeping better and that was apparent in so many ways. He looked like her Hamish again. Not the tired, distant stranger who had been inhabiting her son's body since Mark's death. No, her beautiful son was returning.

She had noticed he was taking time to sit in silence for a few minutes several times a day, and the look of serenity that she observed on his face at these times was a pleasure for a concerned mother to behold. Her Hamish was returning and the thought made her heart swell with love. He had even become interested in his studies again.

This practice called 'mindfulness' seemed to be working so well for him. Monica decided to look into it herself. Perhaps they could both do a course or go on a retreat. She had heard of mindfulness retreats. She would speak to Hamish about it, but for now it was enough to know her son was definitely on the road to recovery.

* * *

Life just seems to have a way of continuing on whether you are ready for it or not, and the Fredrick family had no other choice than to settle into their new kind of dysfunctional normal.

For Christine, it was not easy. She had begun the process of her own healing that day, outside the school, amidst the sound of screeching brakes and the smell of rubber that subsequently assaulted her nostrils, after tyres burned hot on bitumen as she had attempted to bring her two-tonne vehicle to an immediate halt. The velocity of the forward motion, interrupted by her braking, had sent her body flying forward and just as suddenly, flung her heavily back into her seat, taking her breath away.

She had sat so winded in her vehicle that day, looking directly into the eyes of a child. A child she had nearly killed through her own negligence. The image of that horrified young boy's eyes fixed on her own, combined with the memory of that terrifying sound of screeching brakes just before the seemingly inevitable impact, would never leave her. The horrendous incident that had come so close to happening was unthinkable.

She knew she had been given a second chance at life on that day and she decided in that pivotal moment, that she would take it with both hands. This had been her wake-up call, when all she still had to lose flashed before her eyes; a single solitary moment of complete clarity that had altered everything.

In that split second, she knew things had to change.

Christine finally decided to get some help in the form of counselling.

It was a hard decision for her to make because she still felt a massive responsibility for failing to protect her only son in the most important of ways, when it counted the most. Her therapist was trying to assist her in finding ways to forgive herself for what she had previously seen as 'the unforgivable.' She was seeking help, for her children, if not for herself, because she knew beyond a shadow of doubt, there was one thing she could never have forgiven herself for; the incident that she had almost caused that day outside the school.

Day by day, little by little, it appeared Christine was reconnecting to life. She had stopped drinking altogether: the thought of it now horrified her. She had returned to doing many of her previously abandoned motherly duties, but there was definitely something that was still noticeably different. She had lost her zest for life. She felt empty inside, as though she no longer possessed the ability to truly feel happy. She was just going through the motions, but even this was an improvement on what she had become since Mark's death.

Alex had been happy to see his beautiful wife attempting to pull herself out of the darkness that she had inhabited for the last seven months, and attempt to return to him and the family, but he could see the truth. They could all see it. This emerging person was a different Christine; an irreversibly damaged version. Somehow the same, yet somehow so extremely altered. *How could she not be?* Alex had initially thought. They had *all* been damaged in some way from this tragedy. He had tried to ignore it at first in the hope that counselling would assist her. It certainly appeared to be helping in many ways, but no matter what he had tried, he still could not connect with her. She seemed distant and cold.

To the outside world, she looked as though she was moving on from the catastrophe that was Mark's death, and this suited many people. Friends, school teachers, even her work colleagues did not know how to reach the other Christine who had been so desperately lost in her own grief. Many people just don't know what to say, and it can often feel so uncomfortable.

Christine had noticed how this experience had changed and negatively impacted so many relationships, in ways that were seen and unseen. People had begun to stay away or completely avoid the topic of how things were going. This didn't really bother her. She didn't want to talk about her precious son with people who thought that her grief had an expiration date. She had wondered what people thought was the correct 'time' allowed to grieve the loss of the child you had carried, loved, cherished and nurtured through every day of his life for eighteen years.

She had allowed herself to become so disappointed with some people she thought had been her friends, that she had often pondered this very question. Exactly how long was this 'supposed' to take? When was she 'supposed' to feel better? Was it two months, or four? Perhaps it was six, and, what was 'supposed' to happen on that very day as midnight heralded the new date that signalled everything 'should' now be okay? She did not know how any of this could ever be measured. Grief, she had learned, was never a one-size-fits-all.

She tried not to judge these people whom she had once considered friends. She did not possess the energy to spend on them and so it didn't really bother her when they began to stay away. She wondered if she herself would have done the same, back in the days when she too was innocent of heart and unable to understand the wrenching pain and despair that comes with great loss.

Christine knew that as time moved on, many people would choose not to talk about 'it', either for their own reasons, or because they didn't want to upset or remind the person grieving of her loss. This concept had always intrigued her. She had considered the possibility that at some point there might be a time, even an hour, that she *did not* think about Mark.

The few social occasions that Christine *had* found herself in during the months that followed were enlightening. She had noticed many people dutifully attempted to avoid the topic, pretending it had not happened although she knew they were all thinking the same thing.

'Don't mention the dead kid,' 'Oh, is that the mother?' 'God how horrendous!'

'Oh, don't stare,' on and on and on it went.

She could hardly blame them. Perhaps she would have been the same, but it was quickly becoming apparent it was better for her to stay home.

She had noticed the discomfort that was often present in these situations. A hesitancy for people to talk to her. There always seemed to be a very large elephant in the room, so to speak; that is until the unavoidable would inevitably happen. Someone would make an inappropriate comment, like, "Oh, I could just kill my son," or "My God boys can be so annoying," or even the mention of another child who had taken his own life.

These faux pas would always be followed by a slightly longer than necessary awkward silence as all eyes dart toward her, the grieving parent, for a split second only, after which someone generally blushes and then someone else quickly changes the subject. Yes, Christine learnt very quickly that most people just don't know what to say.

Bearing this in mind, Christine just smiled her way through all the necessary social situations. School pick-up, coffee with her best friend Cathy, or even discussions with her work colleagues about when she may return, and all the while never a word was spoken about Mark.

There were some people who surprised her, however. People whom she hardly knew, or who she had not spoken to in a long time who did reach out and asked her how she was coping, but she would not let them in.

"I'm doing better, thank you for asking," was the usual prepared reply.

Her grief was personal. She knew that there were mothers at the school who talked about her behind her back. She knew there were others that judged her in some way for letting this happen. What kind of a household must she have been running for something so terrible to have taken place? There were those who were ever ready to judge and criticise, and so Christine kept to herself. She wasn't ready to let anyone in yet. How could she trust anyone else when she could not trust herself, and so she continued on, outwardly appearing to be improving, but inwardly she was just going through the motions.

The people around her were happy to see signs of her moving forward, but only Alex really knew that the Christine whom he was now living with in their family home was not *his* Christine. Yes, she had stopped drinking. Yes, she was now doing everything expected of her. Yes, she certainly looked like his Christine, but she was not. This Christine was distant and emotionally cold, and he could not connect to her no matter how he tried.

He had attempted to move back into their marital bedroom, but Christine had not wanted this. She had insisted that it was too soon and he needed to stay in the spare room where he had been sleeping for all these months. Yes, he knew; things were indeed different.

* * *

Alex had made the choice to stay based in Melbourne. Over the last month he had noticed a change in his boss that was beginning to indicate that the great man may well have changed his mind about Alex taking over the international running of the firm. He was certain that this change of heart was intricately linked to the fact that Huckett now considered Alex to be damaged goods. Alex would need to 'prove himself' once again to earn back the trust of Huckett, but this did not bother Alex in the least. He made his own choices for his own reasons, independent of the thoughts and opinions of Stewart Huckett, and independent of the implications of the P.T.S.D. he had experienced in the form of panic attacks.

He now had no concern whatsoever about flying. He was able once again to think about flying without any discomfort at all. In fact, his therapist had already taken him on several virtual flights during his deep hypnotic sessions. He felt completely at ease and peaceful during the experience, his sense of "normal" as far as flying went, had returned.

It was none of these reasons that had caused Alex to reconsider his future at the firm, when he graciously declined the promotion; something he believed he would never do. Alex now recognised his priorities had changed.

His family were too important to him. If Christine was to continue on her current path, the need for him to be there for his girls was even more important. It was no longer an option for him to leave; he was choosing his family, he needed to be close to his girls during this time of healing, for all their sakes.

* * *

Jessica had struggled along on her own in the months that followed Hannah's improvement. She felt that she could finally step back a little from the self-imposed role of Hannah's protector. There was a part of her that was in some way relieved that her father and Hannah had managed to find some common ground on which to move forward together, but there was another part of her that felt somehow alone.

She was not at all sure what to think, feel or believe about what she had been told by each of them about Mark. She was just happy that their belief, real or not, was helping Hannah and her dad to heal from their respective griefs. She would have loved that indulgence, but she truly believed that for her, indulgence was exactly what it was. After all, her father and her sister were both trying to deal with the overwhelming grief and trauma of this event. Neither of them could hold themselves responsible for Mark's death as she herself was, she reasoned. This fact alone meant to Jessica that they were free to heal, free to move forward in any way they could, and this is exactly what they were doing. She, on the other hand, was dealing with something else. Something that would never go away: her own guilt.

She was now struggling with an increased sense of isolation induced by the developing dynamics within the Fredrick household, compounded by her enormous guilt and grief, and found herself reaching out for help in unexpected places. She had been skipping meals, which in some way gave her a misplaced sense of control. The hunger she experienced was also an added bonus, a form of self-flagellation, or appropriate punishment for her perceived wickedness for what she had allowed to happen on that day. However, this was no longer enough.

Prior to this occasion she had never drunk alcohol and had never taken drugs of any kind. She was often the butt of many jokes from other students who considered themselves to be more worldly. They were the risk takers, and they enjoyed the notoriety that came when others knew it too. Drug taking was as far from who Jessica really was, as you could possibly get, yet when one of these risk takers, who regularly indulged in these practices at parties, offered Jessica something to ease her pain, Jessica said yes. She no longer cared that this was dangerous; she just wanted the pain and guilt to stop, and stop it did, for a while at least, but not in the way she had hoped.

The designer drug with the promise that she would feel amazing in no time, had been obtained from overseas. As with all drugs of this nature, nobody really knew what was in them, or what effects any given batch would produce on a young body, but Jessica threw caution to the wind. She had been the good girl, she had tried to live up to the world according to perfect Mark Fredrick, but not any more. Here she had been offered relief at last, something that was sure to make her feel better, and she took it.

It was late after school one Friday evening, when Jessica and the other students who were about to participate in this little bit of rebellion and fun, gathered together in the school grounds. Jessica was feeling nervous and nearly did not go ahead with it, but she was cajoled into it by the all-knowing, those students who had each done such things many times. She was never one to give in to peer group pressure but this was indeed, for the first time ever, exactly what she was about to do. The scored tablet that she was given was small and white. She held it in her hand and stared at it as a feeling of anxiety spread through her core. A feeling of panic grew within her and she just wanted all of these feelings to finally stop. Without thought, her hand went to her mouth and she swallowed the tiny tablet that had promised so much. Not long after that, everything began to fall apart.

This could kill me! Do I really want to die? What if this kills me? She began to feel panic, as her mind started running wild. *How will my family cope if I die? Oh my God, I'm such a terrible person!*

The worry that instantly overwhelmed her was not about herself but about Hannah, and her parents. At this point in time she really didn't care if she died, but she didn't want her family to suffer any more. Suddenly, she thought of her grandparents, what would they think, *oh my God what have I done?* Her heart started to race; panic overcame her. Her friends could see her distress and tried to calm her. They sat her down on the grass, just behind the multi-purpose room, out of sight of any teachers that may be lurking about after hours, and hidden from street view, but it was too late. This ride had officially left the platform and there was nowhere to get off now and nothing else for her to do but hold on. *She did not want to die. Why had she agreed to this?* Her heart beat sounded in her own head as though it was going to explode. She could not think clearly. There was a nausea that was developing in her stomach. She was scared and her anxiety was growing with every breath. She felt out of control. *Was this how it was all going to end for her?* She remembered saying "Help me," to one of the girls, who was looking pretty scared herself at the sight of Jessica. That was the last thing she remembered before she passed out. Perhaps she had fainted, perhaps it was something else, but her head hit the ground with a thud and tilted to one side. She vomited the contents of her stomach as her body desperately tried to expel the toxic irritant.

The other students scattered.

"She'll be fine," one said as she ran off, and perhaps she really wanted to believe that.

"Let's go now!" said another, fearful at what he was observing right in front of him.

"Nobody say a fucking thing about this," said a third as they all disappeared and left Jessica unconscious, unable to fend for herself.

All, that is, except for one student who would not leave. This student had not taken the designer drug. She had pocketed it and pretended she had taken it. She sat with Jessica, rolling her onto her side, ensuring she did not choke on her own vomit. She looked at the large amount of vomit that Jessica was now lying in. "Good," she said tenderly, as she tucked Jessica's vomit-splattered slightly matted hair back behind her ears.

"She'll wake up soon," she thought to herself.

This student was Melissa Crompton, youngest of four, whose own brother had died from a drug overdose. She knew what to do; she had done it before. She dialled the number.

Help arrived as Jessica was coming too. Fortunately, she had not ingested much of the substance before her own body expelled it for her. Reality struck her hard as she realised what had nearly happened.

The help that arrived was Melissa's older brother. Ben, a paramedic, was very used to dealing with drug overdoses, but he was not at work now. He administered Jessica with all the necessary fluids and an opioid antagonist to reverse the effects of any opioids that may have been in her system.

"Good job, Sis," he said to Melissa. "There's a really bad batch on the streets at the moment. You may have just saved her life."

He was confident and gently spoken, as he said, "You are going to be okay, Jessica."

"Is there someone we can call for you?"

"No," a still very groggy and disoriented Jessica replied as she was slowly returning to consciousness. She couldn't tell her parents; her mother would never cope. Not Dad or Hannah either.

"Grandparents?"

"No. I really don't want anyone to know about this. You can't tell them, please don't tell them." She began to cry as reality was setting in.

She also realised in that moment that she had not cried for a very long time. It felt good to let it out.

The effects of the drug she had taken were slowly wearing off, but not quickly enough.

"I can't just let you go without proper supervision, Jessica. You either let me take you to the hospital to get checked, or the only other alternative—and trust me, I don't do this for anyone else—is that you come back to our place for the night, so we can keep an eye on you. It's that or I'll have to tell your parents; but given your circumstances, I'm thinking that is not the best option at the moment."

She had given herself a fright today, and she was still feeling worse for wear. Going to hospital was out of the question, but the thought of not having someone around to help her in case she needed it, was something that scared her more. She decided that she would spend the night at Melissa's.

"What about your parents?" Jessica asked.

They will be fine, we'll just tell them you are sleeping over. Here's my phone, call your parents."

* * *

Mark and Grace stood aside as Ben and Melissa tended to Jessica. He did not enjoy seeing the constant and unrelenting ripples of his actions that were now so long ago. He had no idea of the far-reaching implications of a single moment in time. He remembered the dreadful feeling of regret he had felt as soon as his feet left the stool, and he wondered now; would he do the same again, given the chance, or would he let that terrible moment pass? What would have happened if only he had reached out for help from his mother or his father? What if he had told someone, anyone, Hamish or even Mr. Preston. How many things would be different? He wondered if Mr. Fryer would still be alive, or if his father would have the promotion he had worked a lifetime to achieve. Yes, things would be very different, he thought.

He whispered to his sister: " *I am so, so sorry, Jess.*"

* * *

Jessica felt a sudden warmth spread through her chilled body. She felt a strange sensation, almost as though she could sense her brother around her. She actually looked around to see if she could see him, but of course, he was not there. She felt silly. The drugs must be affecting her she thought as she looked at Ben. Ben, this confident, competent paramedic packed up his equipment and prepared to help her to his vehicle. He had come here, to this hidden spot behind the multi-purpose room just for her; to care for her. As she regarded this young man she thought again of her own brother, and how much she missed him. In that moment she almost thought she could hear his voice saying, *"I'm so, so sorry Jess."* She smiled at the memory of him.

It must have been the wind.

Jess stayed that night at Melissa's place. Ben, who often stayed at his girlfriend's, decided to take a night off and spend some time at his parent's house. He had taken a big risk in not reporting this to the school and to Jess's parents, and on any other occasion he most certainly would have, but Melissa had given him the background story, and he thought that this family had suffered enough. In return for his discretion, Jessica had promised to speak with the school counsellor first thing Monday morning, and Ben was going to ensure she did.

Monday morning arrived and Jessica did as she had promised. She made an appointment to speak with the school counsellor to discuss the darkest of secrets that she could not tell another living soul; that she had walked away when her brother needed her the most. That she, Jessica Fredrick, was responsible for the death of her brother.

She was glad that Ben had insisted that she seek help. As much as she did not want to tell anyone of her guilt, the mere act of speaking about that terrible day and her part in it felt like a weight had lifted from her shoulders. It did not take away the guilt, but it did give her hope.

The counsellor was Gaia Solomon; a life saver in a stormy sea of emotional turmoil. Gaia threw Jessica a life vest and Jessica grabbed hold tight. She felt she could almost begin to float again. She had become so exhausted swimming against the tide, all alone for so long, that she did not know how much longer she would have been able to stay afloat. She clung to the security of Gaia's wisdom and reassurance, and ever so slowly Jessica discovered that she could begin to find a safe harbour from her damaging thoughts. The guilt began to lessen as Jessica was taught to look at things from a new perspective. The pain and the grief that comes with the loss of a brother would not go away, but Gaia was teaching Jessica how she could move forward and begin to live with it.

It was at this point that things for Jessica began to turn around. She had felt a real connection to this woman who had already begun to make a significant difference in her life. She agreed to continue seeing Gaia at least weekly for the rest of the year. She would learn how to process her guilt and how to live with her grief. It was a start.

* * *

Christine had carried on bravely since the unfortunate near incident outside the school. She had attended counselling for a while but had since stopped. She found the process futile; after all, no amount of talking was going to bring her son back. She had changed a good many things, but the one thing that seemed impossible for her to change was the enormous pain and responsibility she still carried for her inability to protect her own son.

She had fairly successfully stepped back into her 'functional' role as mother in the Fredrick household, but that was where it ended. She couldn't bring herself to rebuild her fractured relationship with Alex. She had wanted to try, and perhaps she did for a while, but to no avail. It was as though something within her had shattered into so many tiny pieces that day in March that it was now impossible to be put back together.

She could not go back to life as normal without her son. She was also beginning to realise that she could now no longer live in the family home. She needed to leave this place that had been a home for their family in happier times. She could not walk past Mark's room without feeling a sense of panic and dread. She had tried to stay, she wanted to, for the sake of the happier memories, but it was as though all those memories had been expunged in one fell swoop on that fateful day. She really had no idea what the future held for her and her husband, but what she did know was that she could no longer live in this house.

Christine picked up the mobile phone and dialled the number that she had not dialled for what seemed an eternity. "McGregor's Real Estate, how can I help you?" A friendly voice answered the phone.

She had not been back since Mark's death. She knew now she would probably never go back to that life that had so consumed her, that place where she couldn't see what was right before her eyes.

"It's Christine Fredrick here, I want to sell my house. Please ask John to come around with the paperwork," was all she could say before abruptly hanging up the phone. There, she had done it; the beginning of the end. She thought she should really feel something sad or nostalgic, but the truth was that she felt nothing, not even relief. However, she knew that anything had to be better than living in this hell.

She would break the news to Alex and the girls when they got home.

17

THE BEGINNING

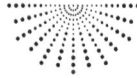

The Fredrick family home had been an easy property to sell. Christine had allowed her colleagues to handle all the details. The thought of managing it herself was almost as intolerable as the reality of continuing to live in the house that now held so many painful memories; memories she could never expunge.

The fractured remnants of her family life were unrecognisable from what they had been nearly twelve months earlier. However, as much as Christine had resisted it, little by little and day by day they were all in their own way coming to terms with a life without Mark.

Alex had desperately tried to rebuild their marriage, but Christine had been unable to let him in. There was just no room for happiness or comfort in those early months; her whole world was so filled with guilt, which only compounded her unrelenting grief. Try as she may, and she did try, she continued to hold herself responsible for Mark's death.

She often wondered what he would be doing now if he were alive. Would he be attending the National Athletic Championships or even preparing for the Olympics? Would he be at University? Perhaps, he would have had a gap year and travelled the world. The thoughts were bittersweet. She loved to get lost in the fantasy, imagining him moving on in his life. It was her one way to still connect with him, to pretend even for a brief moment that he was still alive. However, whenever she allowed herself such indulgences the reality of life soon came crashing down around her. Her Mark would never travel the world. Her Mark would never go to the Olympics, have a gap year or get a job. He would never fall in love, get married, or give her the blessing of a grandchild. Her Mark would do none of these things, and, for the life of her, she still couldn't come to terms with why? Why did he have to do what he did? Why couldn't he have reached out to her? Why didn't he ask for help? Why hadn't she seen he was so troubled? Why? Why? WHY?

Alex, who could no longer bear to see Christine just going through the motions of a numb existence, had regretfully agreed to move out when the house was sold. He still held hope that one day he would find his Chris again, but for now, for all of their sakes, he would give her the space he felt she needed to heal. He would tell the girls it would not be forever, and he truly hoped with all of his heart that this was true, although a part of him was not so sure.

As Christine settled into her bed in her new house on that first night, a house which she could not yet think of as home, her last thoughts were of Mark before the exhaustion of the moving day took its toll.

* * *

Mark looked on as his exhausted mother drifted off to sleep. He wanted to hold her in love and let her know the truth as he was now coming to know it. He moved closer.

"Mum," he whispered gently.

His mother stirred in her dreamlike slumber, her subconscious mind becoming aware of her son's presence.

"Mark?" she whispered as a sleepy smile formed on her slumbering face.

"Mum, it's me. I'm here. I need to talk to you Mum. You can hear me, can't you?"

Again Christine's slumbering countenance expressed the slightest of smiles that indicated that she was hearing her son.

"I'm sorry, Mum. I made a grave mistake, but it was my mistake, not yours. You must let go of the guilt, Mum. It was never yours to hold," he said reassuringly.

"The love is here, Mum, it doesn't end. I can still feel it." Again he paused hoping that his message was being received.

"I love you, Mum," he finally said as Christine drifted back into quiet slumber.

* * *

The next morning Christine arose after the best night's sleep she had had since the death of her son.

There was something different in the air. She couldn't quite put her finger on what it was, but she could feel it. The tiniest of shifts... perhaps it was the new house, a sense of a new beginning; she wasn't sure—but there was a lightness about her, and, for the first time, she felt she could breathe without the heavy weight that had been pressing down on her since that terrible day.

Jessica and Hannah, having heard the movement of their mother, came into the kitchen for breakfast.

"Good morning girls, how did you both sleep?"

"Good, thank you Mum," Hannah replied. "But my mattress feels funny."

"I'll have a look at it, love. I'm sure it will settle, it's just because we have moved it. What do you want for breakfast?" Christine asked as she returned to stacking the dishes in their new kitchen.

"That's what Mark said," Hannah whispered, but nobody heard her words over the sound of the clatter of plates.

"Sorry, Jess, what did you say?" Christine added.

"I'll have cereal."

"Okay, easily done," Christine replied as she handed Jess a bowl and the milk carton.

Hannah, who had found the bread and the toaster, had already put in two slices for herself and was now searching the cupboards for the peanut butter.

"I had the strangest dream last night," Jessica blurted out without thinking. She had already consumed a bowl of cereal and was in the process of pouring herself another.

"Really? What was your dream about, Jess?"

This time Jessica thought before she spoke. She was not sure how her mother would feel about what she had to say. Her mother seemed to be in good spirits today for the first time in a long time, and Jessica didn't want to spoil that.

"Oh, nothing important," she eventually said.

"Oh, come on Jess; you can tell us," said Hannah, knowing if her sister had brought it up she must want to talk about it. "Tell us!"

"Yes, Jess; tell us," parroted Christine.

Jessica looked back at the two expectant faces.

Christine continued stacking the cupboards until Jessica eventually began to talk.

"I dreamt about Mark," she finally said. "I dreamt he sat with me and told me that I should be in the school production, and he wanted me to be in it next year. It was weird."

Christine had her back to the girls, stacking plates, when Jessica spoke; neither girl could see the look of shock on her face, they could only hear the sound of crockery shattering as the plate that Christine had been holding slipped from her grip and fell to the tiled floor.

"Mum, are you okay?" Jessica asked.

Christine turned around, her face white, as the dream that she herself had had last night instantly flooded back into her conscious awareness.

"Oh my God!" she stammered.

"I'm sorry, Mum," Jessica murmured, immediately regretting her words. "I shouldn't have said anything."

Hannah looked surprised at all the fuss. "He *was* here last night." She candidly said as she collected the dustpan to clean up the mess.

"What?" both Jessica and Christine chimed simultaneously as they turned to see Hannah leaving the room.

"Dad knows he comes," she innocently replied.

"I'm sorry, Mum," said Jessica, ignoring her little sister.

"I dreamt about him last night too, Jess. I had forgotten all about it until you said something. I dreamt he told me he loved me and it wasn't my fault." Christine slowly replied as she began to vividly recall the details of her own dream.

"Mum, I dreamt he told me that too," Jessica replied.

Christine slipped into the nearest seat. Mother and daughter stared at each other as the broader implications of this coincidence began to dawn on them both.

"I heard a noise in his room that day, and I never went in," Jessica finally confessed as tears that she had held for nearly a year spilled forth. "I could have saved him, Mum, but I didn't. I didn't go in. I even hoped he was going to get into trouble for once. But I didn't know, Mum. Honestly I didn't know. I thought he had spilled something on the carpet. I'm so sorry, Mum. I could have saved him but I didn't, I just kept walking."

"Oh Jess, my darling girl, of course you didn't know, nobody knew. It wasn't your fault, sweetheart. It was never your fault. None of us wanted this to happen, but it did happen. I am so sorry you have had to carry the weight of these thoughts all alone for all these months. I'm so sorry I have not been here for you." She stood and reached for her daughter and embraced her tenderly as Jessica's tears of relief flowed freely. At last she had said the words she had been too afraid to say.

Hannah joined the group hug too.

When they separated Christine quietly said, "In my dream Mark said to me that he chose this and it was nobody's fault."

For the first time Christine could smile as she thought of her immensely talented son. She hugged her daughters again.

* * *

Mark's last moments with his benevolent celestial guide Grace, who had been with him for every moment of this incredible journey, were poignant. Now it was time for him to truly understand just what this had all been about.

As he turned his attention toward her majestic ethereal presence for the last time, she radiated an intensified loving glow that engulfed him too. Just when he wondered how it could be possible for him to feel any greater love, he found himself completely immersed in her heightened loving energy in all of its entirety.

Mark felt so humbled by her grace that it suddenly became apparent: he now understood that her name was not who she was, but rather what she was. She was the personification of pure grace and she was the purest form of love. In this moment, there was no separation between them.

He instinctively knew who and what he was. No longer was he eighteen-year-old Mark Fredrick; he was an eternal soul who had inhabited many lifetimes and who possessed the wisdom of the ages. He was a part of everything, and everything was a part of him. In this moment he was pure consciousness and he had access to all universal wisdom, all universal knowledge and all universal potential.

Grace explained to him that everything we do on this earthly plane has a vibration that creates a ripple through time and space that touches and affects many people as it spreads far and wide.

"Humans are here on this Earth to experience this life through their senses, to be kind to one another, to love and be loved, and to grow and learn what you need to learn. You can never know the full extent of the impact of your ripple while you are here on Earth; and, as you can see, it is often underestimated. You can never really know how much you are loved, and whose lives you have touched and affected throughout your journey. There are no isolated events; everything and everyone is connected. It is the *illusion* of separation that creates hatred of others, or self-loathing; but, truly Mark, there can be no hatred, there can be no self-loathing, when you genuinely recognise the truth. We are all connected, and all there really is, is love. It is the heart that beats within every sentient being. It's the purest, most elevated emotion. It connects you to all things. Even when you are not aware, you are loved eternally and completely—and you are never alone. I have been with you since before the moment of your birth, and I will be with you for a long time yet to come."

"I wonder what a difference this would make to your world if people really knew this, Mark?"

"How different your world would be, if people recognised and understood that we are all part of a greater source and we are all connected. If humanity understood that there is no separation, there would be no wars, there would be no hatred, there would be no greed. The love you have experienced here is always with you, because there is no separation. Separation is an illusion. You can see how everything was affected by the choices you made; choices that created a ripple so far reaching that the enormity of it was often hidden from view."

"Did you ever have any idea of just how loved and respected you were?"

"Know this Mark, I have always been with you, not in this form, but in the form of a butterfly that flutters past you on a still day; in the form of an eagle in the sky when you are in need of inspiration; in the form of a colourful rainbow lighting up a darkened wintry sky, when all you can see is grey. Solace can be found everywhere. I am there whenever you think of me; but you must look for the signs, Mark. When you think of me, I am there. Love is always there and love is all there is. God is love and love is God. All other emotions are nothing more than an illusion to keep you stuck in fear—and fear will always prevent you from reaching your true potential. Now you see, we all create our own reality. Whatever you look for in this earthly realm, you will certainly find. When you look for and notice heartache, you will find heartache. When you look for fear you will find fear around every darkened corner—but when you look for and tune into love, love is what you discover. It's all around you."

"When you tune into love you are tuning into your true potential."

"You have now observed just what can be achieved, and what can be just as easily lost, by noticing what has happened to those who loved you since you left. The students at your school came together in love to create a better world; the effects you had on those you loved the most, and the effects on those you never even knew. Now you see the truth Mark, all of this has happened—yet none of this had to happen.

Time is not as you know it or understand it to be. Time is not linear; every possibility exists."

"The responsibility for the choices you make is yours and yours alone."

"Now that you know that you create your own reality, Mark, I wonder what you would choose if you had your time again, now that you truly know the choice is always yours? Would you choose to use what you have learned to make a difference in the world, or would you choose to make the same choices? You may be discovering that, when you make the same choices, nothing ever changes. Everyone creates their own reality; most people just don't understand that."

"You always have the choice to act with love or to act with fear."

Grace let that last message sink in for a moment.

She turned again to Mark. "You have now seen your ripple; this was never meant to be your time, and now you have the precious gift of wisdom that has spoken to you and shown you just how important, needed, and loved you truly are."

"I wonder what you would choose if you had your time again?"

Mark Fredrick was resolute. He knew with such conviction that he would never have made that same choice again. He longed to be able to go back to that pivotal moment, knowing what he now knew, but he was sadly aware that he would never have such an opportunity. The finality of his choices hung heavily in the air.

"If only I had known," he said as he looked remorsefully towards Grace. "I am truly sorry."

"Please forgive me."

His heart was so heavy with regret that, in that very moment, he could actually feel all the pain he had caused, and it was intolerable. "It's all my fault, everything that happened. I created it all."

Grace's loving energy field expanded even further as she said, "Mark, you are responsible for your actions only. What others choose is a part of their own journey. You are not responsible for the choices of others. How you respond to anything in the earthly realm is what truly defines you." She looked toward him with benevolence.

"Forgiveness is already yours, Mark...come with me now...it's time for us to go home."

* * *

9:30am Tuesday the 18th March.

It was exactly one year to the day since Mark's death had rocked her world. Christine Fredrick stood on the stage of the auditorium at the Green Valley Secondary College. She cleared her throat and prepared for what she sensed would be the most important speech of her life.

Jessica sat up the front with Nanna Rose and Grandma Mary by her side, and even Hannah had been allowed to miss school for the day so she could attend. All knew they were there to support Christine and honour Mark. All eyes were on Christine, as they waited expectantly.

Things had changed for Christine since that first night in their new home. She truly believed that Mark had visited her that night to relieve her of her guilt, but she also believed there was another reason. She had discovered something else that night that would help her heal—a sense of purpose. She would create something of value from the ashes of utter despair. A legacy of sorts. Her precious son's legacy. She would use her experience to help others. To tell her story and to speak openly about the impacts of suicide, with the sole purpose of creating awareness that may possibly save lives.

The hall fell silent. Christine looked at her girls sitting in the front row. She felt a resolve growing deep within her. She must do this right, for her son and importantly, for any child struggling with mental health issues.

"Good morning staff, students and parents. I am Christine Fredrick. Most of you may know me or know of me, I am the mother of Mark Fredrick, whom I'm sure you all remember." Christine paused in front of the sea of sad faces.

"Today I'm here to talk to you about the topic that, over the past twelve months, I have learned not many people want to talk about. I'm here to talk openly and honestly about suicide."

She paused as murmurs rippled through the auditorium.

"Mark made the *second worst* choice of his entire life when he chose to keep the fact that he was struggling all alone with the pressures of modern life, compounded by the relentless impacts of cyber bullying, to himself. Mark chose this, despite the fact he had a loving support system all around him. He never asked for help, and, because of that, my life, and the lives of all those who loved Mark, will never be the same again. On this day, exactly one year ago, my son—your school captain—made the *worst choice* of his entire life. Mark, my beautiful boy, made a choice that day to end his pain and anguish. You see, Mark was successful at many things, he was an athletics champion, popular and loved. He was surrounded by friends and family; but my son, for all his successes, with all his supports, still chose to end his pain by ending his life. If it can happen to him, then surely it can happen to anyone," Christine warned, feeling her own voice waver slightly. She paused a moment to regain her composure.

"Today I stand before you to pledge my determination to do all that I can to ensure all the Marks in the world know there are other choices. I want to speak openly about the reality of suicide. believe me, it isn't pretty or glamorous; it is damaging, painful and relentless. It never goes away. Each and every day my family and I have to live our lives without Mark, and trust me when I say, there are days I have not wanted to do that. There were days I hid away from the world. Months that I retreated into the numbing effects of alcohol. Days I did not want to go on living. My entire family struggled with the greatest tragedy that any of us had ever had to endure; nobody was spared."

"Each of us had blamed ourselves in some way for the things we could have, should have or would have done—if only we could have known— we became tormented by the things we did not know, or say, at the time. Each of us was grieving this enormous loss in our own way, and the only thing that kept us all going—and still keeps us all going—is each other. We are all each other's lifelines, and when one of us loses our grip on the flotation device and threatens to fall into the abyss of despair, there is someone there to grab our exhausted hand and drag us back to safety. Without my family, I really don't know what I might have done."

She paused for the impact of her statement to be understood, as she looked at Hannah and Jessica both with tears in their eyes looking back at her.

"My message today is clear; we all need that lifeline when things become intolerable. We all need a helping hand sometimes. We are never meant to travel this difficult world alone. We all need to reach out for help."

"Mark had just wanted his pain to stop, and I can only assume that he felt so burdened thinking he should have been able to cope with life's troubles on his own. Perhaps it wasn't the done thing for a coper, such as him, to ask for help. But I want you all to know: we all need help sometimes. You see, the longer Mark resisted that option, the more he continued to sink deeper and deeper into the destructive aspects of the cyber world; a world that is so damaging. A world that is self-esteem stealing, confidence reducing and artificially edited. A virtual world that leads you further and further away from the real world and real help. Mark's sleep was also compromised, and that's when everything spirals even more out of control. I'm told his lack of sleep would have compounded his existing distress and anxieties as those social media notifications continued to ping all night long, reducing his ability to reason or cope. If only I had known, but I didn't know. I didn't know any of it. I wish I had." She paused.

"I'm sure many of you know the feelings of being addicted to checking in and seeing what people are saying online, often about you, often in the most damaging of ways. Damage is done in the face-less cyber world where people think they have the right to say anything, post anything, true or untrue, as though the recipients of their hurtful taunts are not real people. Well I am here today to tell you, beyond a shadow of doubt, that these people *are real* people, with real feelings and real issues. These are the unedited and un-photoshopped issues that will never be posted in chat rooms for all to see. In the world of 'keeping-up' where everyone appears to be achieving massive successes and nobody is failing at anything—there are so many of you who are not keeping up, who *are* failing, who are not perfectly photoshopped—and who are silently trying to deal with the anxiety and depression caused by a world that feels out of control; a world leaving you far behind."

Christine paused briefly. There was a quiet rustling sound coming from the audience as students shifted in their seats as the uncomfort-able truths began to hit home.

"Mark was a tall poppy, and as such was the recipient of many taunts, but even I had no idea of what he was dealing with, until after his death. If only I had known. It has to stop, and I want all of you to be part of the movement to help it stop. If not out there in the wider world, at least let's start it here in our own community. We *can* make a difference."

Christine looked about the auditorium; she knew she had the full attention of the students and teachers alike. She felt the silent acknowledgment of what she was saying in the gentle nods of agree-ment. Her words were resonating with them.

"My son struggled on alone for as long as he could until the heavy weight of this emotional burden became too much for him to endure.

We have to continue these important conversations as loudly as we can because lives are on the line. No topic is off limits for me anymore. I *will* talk about suicide, I *will* talk about mental health awareness, I *will* talk about the damaging effects of social media misuse and I *will* talk about social drug use—I know there are some of you here today whose brains have been physically changed and damaged by the excessive euphoric stimulation of readily available, and by most, readily acceptable dangerous drugs that forever leave a person feeling heavy with depression and feelings of despair, right? Real life struggles to compete with these enormous artificial highs. Life for those of you participating regularly in these activities—and I know there are many of you here in this hall—can begin to feel like nothing is ever good enough anymore. Yes—I am broaching the silent subject of social drug taking because it is not only contributing to teenage death from overdose and from antisocial behaviours, but is a contributing factor to death by suicide. We need to stop pretending everything is all right, because everything is not all right."

"I want to let you know that you are never alone, even when you feel completely isolated—there is always help available. While you are still alive, there is hope. The sooner you ask for it the sooner you get it. Don't wait till it's too late. Don't wait till you feel there is no other choice because there is always another choice. There is *always* another option."

"Over these last twelve months I have learned that there is so much more to life and to death than you would ever believe: love is the key and love is always the key, and it isn't the love of another, it is a far greater, far more intense love than that; it is the love of the self, the love of the soul. We are a connected community, and it's time to understand that the love and acceptance we are all looking for comes from within. When you love yourself and respect yourself, you can begin to heal from the inside out. When you love yourself and respect yourself, you can love and respect others—it's as simple, yet as complex as that."

"You are not alone—and this, for me, is the most reassuring thing I have ever learned. Be kind to each other, treat each other with respect. How can we hate or hurt another when we are all connected? You are surely only hurting and hating yourself, this is the truth. Importantly, be kind to yourselves, love yourselves enough to raise your hand and ask for help because the thing that you cannot cope with today may feel more manageable tomorrow. Even the heaviest feelings of despair are not so heavy when there are two of you carrying them. I wonder how many of you may have already noticed that?"

"So how do we create change?"

There was silence in the auditorium.

"Let me answer this for you: we create change by doing *something* differently."

"We need to bring mental health issues out into the light, and we do this by being open, being honest, getting real. I have witnessed the massive impact one action can have on thousands of people. What kind of impact do you think we can have when we all work together? Change is possible, and it begins with a simple first step."

"So today I stand before you all, putting it all on the line in the hope that my honesty and my story can inspire some of you to seek help." She paused.

"I am desperately trying to get you all to understand that this is real. My son, Mark Fredrick, your captain, an A grade student, a champion athlete, who had many friends, a loving family, who was surrounded by wonderful teachers and community...killed himself...and nobody saw it coming, not even me."

Instantly, the hall fell silent again. All eyes were upon Christine.

"He killed himself," she repeated, almost in a whisper, as tears welled and her body threatened to betray her, but she stood steadfast resolute in her purpose.

She thought of Mark and continued on.

"Under the wonderful direction of Greg Preston this school has moved forward in the fight against teenage suicide, but we must not become complacent. There are school counsellors at this very school who are not being utilised. As a community we must not slip back into complacency. I know there are people out there in this audience today who are struggling with mental health issues who have not sought help. Please help me today to keep the conversation going and to assist in removing the stigma, in an effort to save lives."

The students looked around the filled auditorium. Christine could feel an undercurrent of energy building as a quiet murmuring began.

"Please," she said with added emphasis, "if this can happen to my son, it can happen to *anyone....*"

"Who of you are suffering silently?"

"Who of you are feeling alone?"

"Who of you are struggling with anxiety or depression?"

"Who of you are struggling with addictions?"

"I stand before you to say that I have been silently suffering; but not anymore. I finally asked for help."

"Who of you are willing to stand with me now and be counted as we begin to create the change we want in our school and in our world?"

The students sat wide-eyed, staring at Christine Fredrick, none prepared to move.

Fifteen seconds seemed like a lifetime to Christine, when from the back of the hall the sound of one lone chair sliding on the wooden floor broke the silence as someone motioned to stand. It was Mr. Lewis, the Year Ten maths and chemistry teacher. The students looked at each other in disbelief; perhaps it was a mistake, perhaps he was just leaving the auditorium—but no, Geoffrey Lewis stood in silence with his head held high, and he looked directly at Christine.

Mr. Lewis was the farthest person anyone could imagine to be struggling with anything, let alone mental health issues. He was the school comedian, always smiling, always cracking a joke. He had all the answers, or so everyone thought. He was often referred to as their very own Robin Williams, the sudden irony of which was not lost on all those looking on.

Then there was movement of another chair, as a Year Eleven girl sheepishly stood, followed by three Year Twelve students; then Mrs. Shingali, school physical education teacher, who had lost her mother to cancer last year. Ms. Pilbrow, the middle school coordinator who had secretly been struggling with infertility was the next to stand, at least a third of the Year Twelve students rose to their feet and very soon nearly twenty percent of the entire student body was standing. One in five students were making a clear statement; they were doing it hard: all standing in silence, all looking at Christine.

In one short address Christine had been able to do what others before her had not. The conversation had once again begun. She looked about the room in silence and slowly nodded her head in acknowledgement as she noticed the collective need for help.

"You are NOT alone," was all she said.

"Thank you all. It is very brave of you to stand up and be counted like this. I want to say to you all that it is okay not to be okay, but today I *strongly* say to you all that it is definitely not okay to struggle in silence. It is not okay to not ask for help. Help is available, and it is time for us all to have a voice. It is time for us to talk openly about coping strategies and interventions at the grass roots level—and that begins here, with each and every one of you."

"I will stand up and talk about suicide, that word everyone shies away from discussing because it is the word we *must* discuss. Did you know that every day at least eight people die from suicide in Australia alone? And did you know that a further thirty will attempt to take their own life...every day? Men are often most at risk because they do not talk about it and don't seek help, so I want to congratulate every one of you standing today. You are brave and you are now part of the conversation, and together we will create change."

"I have spoken to Mr. Preston today and we have agreed that Green Valley Secondary College, on the 18th March every year, will now have a Memorial Day for Mark Fredrick as well as Stacey Wilson. It will be called 'Stand Up for Mental Health Awareness Day.' It will be a day to raise funds for mental health support in our community, a day to remind each and every one of you that you are not alone. It will be a day to remember my son, Mark Fredrick and Stacey Wilson and every other child or adult who have lost their battle against this insidious disease; a day to remember all of the families and friends who have ever been impacted by suicide or mental health issues. Mostly, I hope it will be a day to ask your friends how they are doing and to 'Stand Up' for mental health awareness."

"Thank you for your bravery."

"Today, we are no longer part of the problem."

"Today, we stand united, resilient and steadfast in our resolve to be part of the solution."

The entire auditorium stood and applauded Christine Fredrick.

From the back of the auditorium, Alex Fredrick looked on in silence with tears in his eyes. He had never been more proud of his beautiful Chris than he was at that very moment.

Christine Fredrick's eyes met those of her estranged husband. For the first time since Mark's death she could really see him. She stood transfixed for a moment as she acknowledged Alex with a half-smile, and a gentle nod of her head.

In releasing her guilt she was now becoming aware that she was making room for something else: healing.

It was a start. She would forever grieve the son she had lost, but day by day she was learning how to live with her grief.

Alex returned a slight smile. He too felt a faint feeling of hope rising within him. A half smile was enough...for now.

It was a beginning.

POSTSCRIPT

This book has been challenging to write for many reasons. My purpose in writing it was to raise awareness about the ever-increasing incidence of suicide, particularly by teenagers and males under 25 years of age. I wanted to explore the factors contributing to these disturbing trends, and to shine a light of hope on the resources that are available.

At the time of writing this book, The World Health Organisation stated that almost 800,000 people worldwide die to suicide every year. In writing this book I have tried to illustrate the enormous impact felt by hundreds of people for every one of these 800,000 untimely deaths. Naturally, for every one of these completed attempts there are countless other failed attempts; so when considering the numbers affected by serious mental health issues, I believe we are really only just uncovering the tip of the iceberg.

According to '*Mindframe,*' an Australian national program supporting safe media reporting and suicide communication, in 2018 there were 3,046 deaths by suicide, equating to an average of 8.3 deaths by suicide every day. A staggering *2,320 of these were male, while 726 were female.* In every age category, the rate of male suicide far exceeded that of the female rates. When faced with making sense of these rates, we must ask ourselves the question: are the sex related discrepancies due to the fact that we, as a society, do not encourage men to speak about their feelings?

The intention of this book is to cause no distress to those already grieving and affected by suicide; rather, it is to acknowledge the terrible ongoing and persistent trauma caused by a single calamitous event. In writing this I hope to highlight the often misplaced guilt held by so many, and to explore the possibility of new beginnings when all seems hopelessly lost.

I believe we all possess the potential to create the change we need to turn our lives around. For while there is life, it is never too late. Help is available in so many places, in so many forms.

As a mental health worker, I have personally become concerned by the increasing number of very young children who present to my therapy room struggling with heightened levels of anxiety and depression as they seek to deal with the pressures of modern life. These children are often as young as five and six.

It is my belief that we need to teach our children how to create the tools required to challenge their negative thoughts and grow resilience within themselves in order to survive an ever-changing world. To normalise, instead of pathologise, certain feelings as just part of the human condition, I feel is a great place to start. To educate children and give them the skillset needed to manage situations when adversity strikes—as it inevitably will—and reassure children that it is *normal* to feel sad, angry, depressed or even devastated in difficult situations.

How we teach our children to express their feelings and work through these emotions is so important, and we must remember that children also learn by example. Thus, as a society, I believe we need to become better communicators, better able to express our feelings and to allow for vulnerability in such situations. To do so shows immense strength, not weakness. Most importantly, the message must be clear: it *is* okay not to be okay sometimes—but it is never okay to not ask for help, because you are precious beyond compare; you are loved and you are never alone.

This is not a book designed to create a sense of helplessness or hopelessness; rather, it is a story to create hope, because there are things that *can* be done. This begins with removing the stigma that has been attached to mental illness for far too long. As a population we often openly display our physical ailments, but choose to hide away from sight our mental health issues.

I wrote this book after personally witnessing the ripples of suicide first hand, and the ever present, far reaching impact experienced across an entire country, visited upon so many people, on so many levels, because of the action of one person. A person who felt he had no one to turn to, and who felt that life for him was no longer worth living. The same person who, moments after his attempt to end his life immediately regretted his actions, and desperately sought to get help. Unfortunately for him, and all those who loved him dearly, help did not arrive on time.

Not forty-eight hours after his death I witnessed hundreds of people from across the country gather to honour him and support the family he had left behind. It really struck me at that time that, if only he had known how much he really meant to all these people, would it have made a difference? I wonder what he would have chosen? For me this highlighted the tragedy of a single action, often based on the intense emotional turmoil of a single, critical moment in time. If only he had known that moment would pass. If only he had known how loved, how valuable, how treasured he truly was in those crucial seconds.

Anecdotally, it is interesting to observe the many reports from survivors who say that they immediately regretted the attempt almost as soon as they had taken action.

Disturbingly, suicide is the leading cause of death in the 15- to 19-

year-old age group. In writing this book I wanted to explore why. I interviewed many young teens and adults alike, and discovered many common themes about the issues that are potentially implicated. Issues such as the negative impact of incorrect media or overuse of social media continued to be raised. Another issue that was implicated was the increased availability and acceptability of drug usage and the negative impact that this is having on the brain's 'reward system.' This is resulting in a decreased ability of the users to feel pleasure from 'normal' activities, leading to increased levels of depression in this group. Anxiety, insomnia, low self-esteem and stress were other associated factors that were identified. It was impossible to determine if they were the principal factors or if they were the distressing symptoms originating from the other predictable causes. The latter I believe is probably true.

I know that with awareness we can create change, and it is my hope that this book will contribute to a growing social awareness by creating inclusive discussions about these issues.

As a society, we must banish the stigma that has led to people feeling that they have failed because they have a chemical imbalance in their brain, or because they have not been taught the skills to build the resilience required to bring themselves back from the depths of despair.

Mostly, I believe we need to reconnect with each other. Never before have we experienced a time like this. We are now more connected than at any other time in the history of the world, yet equally ironically, we are now more disconnected. We experience less human contact, less eye contact, less physical human touch and less of the family unit that has traditionally surrounded us. There is now a growing and significant body of evidence that shows the absolute critical importance of all of these factors on the mind, brain and body that are essential for normal human development. Never underestimate the power of a smile or a word of encouragement to change someone's day and possibly save someone's life.

When we begin to truly understand that every single thought we have will be the precursor for immediate chemical and physical change within our body, we can begin the process of healing. For those of you who have lost a loved one, I give you my heartfelt sympathy and ask that you may consider my words, when I suggest that perhaps it is possible to find within yourself an ability to release any emotions that no longer serve you. In exchange for guilt, pain, anger, regret or any other damaging emotion, I say to you, seek love.

Remember the precious memories, remember the love. They are still there, because nothing is ever truly lost in the universe.

I have explored in the pages of this book the possibility of an ever-present and ongoing love that has the ability to heal all. There is so much we are yet to discover, but together we can create change, and together we can save lives.

* * *

If you are in need of support, please contact your local healthcare professional.

* * *

There are crisis assessment teams based in many local hospitals who can respond to mental health crisis 24 hours a day.

In Australia www.healthdirect.gov.au has a list of mental health crisis lines for every state which provides immediate expert support.

If you are struggling with depression it is imperative to seek help, and to have a safety plan prepared with phone numbers readily displayed so you can access resources and connect to immediate help should you require it. A well timed-phone call may save your life.

* * *

There are many wonderful organisations that provide mental health care support to assist people in crisis.

These include, but are not limited to;
Mental Health Foundation of Australia
Youth beyondblue
Beyond Blue
Lifeline
Headspace
Black Dog Institute
Mental Health Australia

DANIELLE AITKEN

Danielle Aitken is an emerging Australian author of contemporary fiction.

.

THE RIPPLES is Danielle Aitken's second book.

Her debut novel was first published in 2018.
'Sarah's Story, Life after IVF'
A story of personal triumph and spiritual growth.

www.danielleaitkenauthor.com.au

facebook.com/daitkenSarahsStory
instagram.com/danielleaitken_author